A COMMENTARY ON
THE NEW
CODE OF CANON LAW

By THE REV. P. CHAS. AUGUSTINE *Bachofen*, O.S.B., D.D.

Professor of Canon Law

VOLUME I

Introduction and General Rules (can. 1-86)

SECOND EDITION

B. HERDER BOOK CO.

17 South Broadway, St. Louis, Mo.
AND
68 Great Russell St. London, W. C.

1918

NIHIL OBSTAT
Sti. Ludovici, die 31 Maii, 1918

> *F. G. Holweck,*
> *Censor Librorum.*

IMPRIMATUR
Sti. Ludovici, die 1 Junii, 1918

> *✠Joannes J. Glennon,*
> *Archiepiscopus*
> *Sti. Ludovici.*

Copyright, 1918
by
Joseph Gummersbach

VAIL-BALLOU COMPANY
BINGHAMTON AND NEW YORK

FOREWORD

Aug. 7th, 1917, the S. Congregation on Seminaries and Studies issued a decree which imposes on teachers of Canon Law the task of explaining the new Code, not only synthetically, but also analytically, by closely following the order and text of the Code itself. The decree also calls for a historical survey, whenever necessary and opportune, of the respective canons. This precisely has been the guiding line along which the writer taught Canon Law at the Benedictine University in Rome for nine years (1906–1915), until the European conflict closed our international College. Most of that time, therefore, fell within the period of the present codification.

We do not intend to make an apology for the commentary now offered to the clergy and all interested in the study of ecclesiastic law. The commentary shall be as brief as the matter permits and shall not be encumbered with moralizing reflections. The reader should remember that the commentary is intended for countries where the English language prevails, and hence for such countries as do not reflect all the customs and laws in vogue and practice elsewhere. Wherefore certain parts of the Code (*e. g.*, cathedral chapters, *jus patronatus*, benefices) will not be treated *in extenso*. We shall endeavor to render the text in a verbal, or at least substantially faithful, transcription, no official English text having reached us. For the rest, the old saw, " Bis dat qui cito dat," has quickened this edition.

THE AUTHOR.

Conception, Mo.

TABLE OF CONTENTS

CONTENTS

THE NEW CODE OF CANON LAW

PART I
INTRODUCTION

CHAPTER I

NAME AND DEFINITION OF LAW IN GENERAL AND CANON
LAW IN PARTICULAR

The Latin word *jus* (from *jurare*, to swear, or *jussum*, command) has a double meaning or sense: a) subjectively, it signifies *right*, or " the moral power to have, to do, or to require something from another (*facultas moralis inviolabilis aliquid habendi, agendi, exigendi*), as we say to give to every one his due (*suum cuique*); b) in the *objective* sense, *jus* denotes norm or *law* either in the singular or plural (complex of laws), for instance, the law of celibacy, civil law, canon law. This latter meaning is attached to the " eternal law," since " the very idea of government of things in God the Ruler of the universe has the nature of a law," [1] and every law, divine or human, is but an irradiance from the eternal law, as all human laws bear the character of laws only in as far as they approach, more or less, this prototype.

Canon Law (jus canonicum, derived from the Greek κάνων, *i. e.* norm or rule), as a technical term occurs since

---

1 *S. Theol.*, I-II, q. 91, a. 1 f.

the twelfth century,[2] this nomenclature being exclusively reserved for the laws of the Church, whilst *lex* (νόμος) was applied to civil laws. Consequently the interpreters of ecclesiastical law were called *canonistae*, those of civil law, *legistae*.

DEFINITION.—Canon Law may therefore be defined as " the complex of rules which direct the exterior order of the Church to its proper end."

EXPLANATION.—a) In this definition the laws of the entire Church only are, *per se*, considered, viz. those laws which touch upon the whole body as such and emanate from the supreme authority (*jus commune*). Hence laws made for a particular portion of the Church or its members are outside our subject except in so far as they form part and parcel of the body of common law. However, since these particular or special rules need the explicit or implicit consent of the supreme lawgiver, and rest on the interpretation of law in general, it is evident that even these particular laws must, to some extent at least, be taken into consideration.

b) The *purpose* of Canon Law, as of all law properly so called, is the establishment and maintenance of *exterior order*. The Church forms an organized body which has its special and proper functions. In a certain sense, she is a body politic with a working to the outside. Hence her laws, either in regard to the hierarchic ramifications, or in relation of member to member, are concerned not directly with internal acts (" *de internis non judicat praetor* "), but with the public or exterior order of the Church at large (*finis proximus juris canonici*).

c) However, the *end* of the *Church* being mainly

2 *Summa Stephani Tornacensis, apud* Schulte, *Gesch. d. Quellen u. Lit. d. can. Rechts*, 1875, I, 29.

spiritual, *i. e.*, of the supernatural order, it is plain that Canon Law must partake of that order, and hence tend, *a potiori*, to a supernatural end. Yet, it is perfectly true what has been said above (b), that ecclesiastical laws are principally intended to maintain the public order, since the Church is not merely a supernatural and an invisible organization, but a visible body consisting of men, not of angels.

Besides the time-honored nomenclature " Canon Law," *i. e.*, the law made up chiefly of canons, there are other names: a) *jus ecclesiasticum*, inasmuch as it embraces the whole range of Church legislation contained in the canons of councils as well as in the decrees and decretals of the popes and in unwritten laws, *i. e.*, legitimate customs; b) *jus pontificium* (a term used *v. g.* by Giraldi), in as far as the supreme and chief source of Church legislation is the Sovereign Pontiff; c) *jus sacrum*, in as far as its main author is Jesus Christ and it treats of sacred persons and things.

DIVISION OF CANON LAW.—a) By reason of its *origin*, Canon Law is either divine or human. *Divine* is that part of it which owes its origin to Christ or the Apostles, in as far as the latter enacted laws by divine inspiration, (which is not, however, to be identified with Scripture inspiration) or promulgated them as divine norms, *v. g.*, the hierarchy, the matter and form of the sacraments (James 5, 14), the *privilegium Paulinum*. *Human* is that portion of the Canon Law which has merely human authority for its existence; thus the Apostolic decrees (Acts XV) are of human authority though established by Apostles; purely human laws, too, are those passed by councils, popes, and bishops, unless, indeed, they are implicitly contained in revelation, or are merely declarations, specifications, or modifications of divine or natural law. In the latter case they belong to the class of divine laws.

b) By reason of its *obligatory force,* either personally or territorially, Canon Law is: α) either *general,* when it binds all members of the Church, or *special,* when it binds only some members or a class of members, *e. g.,* the clergy, regulars; β) either *universal,* when it is incumbent on the entire Church as far as it is spread, or *particular,* when it affects only a certain portion of the Church, as a province or diocese. Under this heading belongs the difference between the law prevailing in the *Oriental*[3] and that binding the *Occidental* Church. γ) By reason of its *promulgation* we speak of written or unwritten law, or custom (*consuetudo*).

d) By reason of *time,* Canon Law is distributed into various epochs: α) *jus antiquum,* or old law, from the beginning of the Church up to Gratian's *Decretum* (about 1150); β) *jus novum,* or new law, up to the Tridentine Council (1545–63); γ) *jus novissimum,* or modern law, up to our time. It remains to be seen whether the New Code will constitute a new epoch.

e) By reason of its *matter,* Canon, like civil law, may be classified into public and private law. *Public* law is concerned with the Church as a society, its government and external relations; *private* law with the rights of the members and their mutual relations.[4]

This latter distinction is rejected by most of the German canonists, *v. g.,* Philips, v. Scherer, Sägmüller, but defended by Roman authors. If we subsume under public law the constitutional law proper, together with that

---

[3] Concerning the laws binding this Church see the *Collectanea Prop. Fid.,* 1907, II, n. 1578; can. I of the *Codex Iuris Can.*

[4] Schenkl, *Institutiones Iuris Eccl.,* 1853, I, § 38, p. 60.

governing the Church's external relations, we believe there is nothing unwarranted in this division. Private law would then embrace chiefly the administrative portion of the laws. Whether we substitute the terms "external" and "internal" is of little importance.

CHAPTER II

THE SCIENCE OF CANON LAW AND ITS IMPORTANCE

Abstracting for a moment from the historical resources, which partly date back to the founder of the Church and partly owe their origin to the natural development of the living organism, Canon Law as a distinct *science* owes its existence and splendor chiefly to the Benedictine monk, *Gratian,* in the middle of the twelfth century, when canonists — and also legists — commenced to cultivate ecclesiastical law systematically.

If science means "a demonstrative syllogism" or conclusions drawn from premises, it is evident that single laws form the stock and store out of which deductions are made, and which, in their turn, may become new laws and new bases for mental operations (*e. g.,* exemption). Science demands a knowledge not only of the several existing laws, but of their systematic and pragmatic putting together. Canonical science must be analytical as well as synthetic, and should be based upon critical and historical researches. And in this latter regard some progress, mainly due to the two brothers Ballerini and to German scholars, has been made.

Preëminently, however, law is *practical,* and hence the canonist should not only know the law, but also be able to apply it to concrete cases, such as occur daily. This is the function of what is called *jurisprudence (juris-*

prudentio sacra), or "the habit (*habitus*) of knowing, interpreting and applying the laws." [1]

As to the *necessity* or *importance* of this systematic-practical science, it is not too much to say that the " watchmen on Sion's tower," *i. e.* the *prelates*, are obliged to possess a more elaborate and extensive knowledge of ecclesiastical laws than is required of the lower clergy. For the prelates should be especially well versed as to the rights of the Church in regard to civil power, and should know the laws regulating their own attitude towards the clergy and the laity. This observation holds good also in regard to the officials of episcopal courts.

The *priests*, too, are bound in conscience to obtain a sufficient knowledge of Canon Law to enable them to discharge their duties as pastors of souls and to defend the rights of the Church and their own position. It is a sad saw, often repeated, " What's the use of Canon Law, the prelate is Canon Law." This saying is not only offensive to the prelates, who are thus represented as arbitrary law-makers and expounders, but betrays a lack of reverence for a noble, time-honored science, and degrades those who utter that unpriestly sentiment to the level of cowards or sluggards. Let them rather hear Gratian: "*Ignorantia mater cunctorum errorum maxime in sacerdotibus Dei vitanda est. Sciant ergo sacerdotes scripturas sacras et canones;*" and again: "*Nulli sacerdotum liceat canones ignorare.*" [2]

In order to make canonical science solid, extensive, and systematic, the canonist, and especially the professor of Canon Law, should be conversant not only with dogmatic and moral theology, but also with Church history and civil law. *History* will render the study of Canon Law

---

[1] Schenkl, *op. cit.,* 41.   [2] C. 4, Dist. 38.

more agreeable, give the student living pictures of the past, and help him to understand many laws otherwise barely intelligible. *Civil Law,* more particularly the old *Corpus Juris Civilis,* will furnish the key to a great many terms, *v. g.,* in civil and criminal procedure, and show the connection existing between civil and religious law. Besides, the priest being a citizen of the State, and, we may justly say, a citizen of higher standing than most others, it appears but just that, even in this respect, his " lips shall keep knowledge, and they shall seek the law at his mouth." [3]   Therefore, in this country, for instance, the Constitution should not be a sealed book to priests, nor should they be strangers to the laws governing marriage, contracts, last will, and labor.

[3] Mal. II, 7.

CHAPTER III

The term *source* or *fountain* of Canon Law (*fons juris canonici*) may be taken in a twofold sense: a) as the formal cause of the existence of a law, and in this sense we speak of the *fontes essendi* of Canon Law or lawgivers; b) as the material channel through which laws are handed down and made known, and in this sense the sources are styled *fontes cognoscendi,* or depositaries, like sources of history.

SECTION 1

Taking for granted that the Church is a complete and autonomous society (*societas perfecta*), she must evidently possess legislative power, *i. e.*, the faculty of enacting laws. For " a law is nothing else than an ordinance of reason for the common good, made by him who has care of the community, and promulgated." [1] Therefore, every law must proceed from the legitimate power residing in that community for which the law is given. Now, the Church Catholic being founded by our Lord and perpetuated by the Apostles and their lawful successors, among whom the Roman Pontiff holds not only an honorary but also a jurisdictional supremacy, the following must be acknowledged as ecclesiastical *lawgivers*:

1. *Christ* our Lord, the original source of divine laws laid down chiefly in the Constitution of the Church, and next to Him the *Apostles* as lawgivers either of divine or human laws, *viz.:* as inspired or merely human instruments.

2. The *Roman Pontiff*, either alone or in unison with a *general council*, as endowed with the supreme and ordinary power of enacting laws for the universal church;

3. The *Bishops* for their respective districts, inasmuch as they are empowered to enact laws subordinate to common law;

1 S, Theol., I-II, q. 90, a. 4.

19

4. *Customs*, too, must be considered as a source of law, universal as well as particular.

Whether the *natural law* can be called a source of Canon Law depends on the formal declaration of the supreme authority; for the natural law as such — its extent is very uncertain — cannot be called a homogeneous source of Canon Law except it has been declared such by the highest authority.[2] Besides its range being very uncertain, the so-called natural law is often nothing but a subjective sentiment, or, at most, a dictate of reason.

2 Cfr. J. Laurentius, S.J., *Institutiones Juris Eccl.*, 1903, p. 9; Schenkl, *l. c.*, 37, justly remarks that the natural law should be cautiously used in Canon Law.

These sources, as we have said, are depositaries in which we find collected the laws enacted in the course of centuries. They may also be considered as the channels through which the river and rivulets of legal enactment flow and are preserved. They do not constitute the law as such, but rather point out where it may be found. Among these sources are Holy Scripture and the decrees of popes and councils; also, in a measure, custom, inasmuch, namely, as it proves the existence and continuity of laws unwritten and perhaps forgotten.

ARTICLE 1

HOLY WRIT

1. When we speak of Holy Writ as a source of Canon Law, it is evident that we refer primarily to the writings of the *New Testament*. There we meet with a nucleus of constitutional laws which were later developed; there, also, are to be found moral precepts which form the connecting link between the Old and New Dispensations.

2. As to the *Old Testament*, a distinction must be made between moral, ceremonial, and judiciary laws. The strictly *moral* laws contained chiefly in the decalogue were received bodily into the New Law. Not so the *ceremonial laws*, which, being ordained for the external worship of God, were modified and even abrogated by the

Church, inasmuch as they were laws of the old Code and to some extent detrimental to the spirit of the universal Church,[1] and consequently have no binding force as laws of the Old Testament (*v. g.*, tithes).

The *judicial* laws of the Old Testament, *i. e.*, those which govern man's relations to other men, were enacted according to the needs of the old theocratic State and have lost their binding force by the coming of Christ. Yet as far as they suit the conditions of the New Testament, they may, not as O. T. laws, but as rules for the N. T., be used even in the Church, because they rest on the dictates of reason[2] (*v. g.*, prohibited degrees of marriage).

ARTICLE 2

DECREES OF THE ROMAN PONTIFFS

The decrees of the Roman Pontiffs have always enjoyed great authority in the Church, from the time of Clement I (+ 100?) to our own day.[3]   Their subject-matter was partly dogmatic, partly disciplinary; it is the latter class that especially concerns Canon Law.

1. It was customary for the Pope, soon after having taken possession of St. Peter's Chair, and on other occasions, to gather a synod in Rome and to send the acts of that synod, together with a profession of faith, to the patriarchs and other prominent bishops.   These documents often contained matter concerning not only the faith but also the discipline of the universal Church, and were called *constituta* (*scil. in synodo*).   Besides, the Popes were often called upon to issue what are called *privilegia,* either for monasteries or for person-

---

1 Cfr. *S. Th.*, I–II, q. 103.
2 *Ib.*, qq. 104 ff.

3 Cfr. Coustant, O.S.B., *Epistolae Rom. Pontificum*, Paris, 1721, a work still useful and highly appreciated.

ages placed in high station. These sometimes bore the character of regular documents (*diplomata*), then again they were but personal letters, though written in a more solemn style, and having a silk thread (*litterae gratiae*) or a hemp thread (*litterae justitiae*) attached to them (eleventh century). Later on, especially under Martin V (1417–31), the custom prevailed in the Roman Curia of distinguishing two principal kinds of papal documents, *i. e., bullae* and *brevia,* which distinction is still preserved. At the time of Innocent VIII (1484–92) another sort of papal letters was introduced, not sealed but only signed by the Pope; their name is "*Motu Proprio*" (*scil. scriptae litterae*). This, in short, is the origin of papal documents.[4]

2. As to the *form* and *juridical value* of the various kinds of papal documents, the following distinctions may serve as a guide:

a) *Bullae, Brevia, Rescripta,* and between the two last-named the so-called "*Motu Proprio.*"

α) *Bullae,* or Bulls, thus called from the seal of lead appended to, or impressed upon, the paper or parchment,[5] and bearing on one side the images of SS. Peter and Paul and on the other the name of the reigning Pontiff, are solemn documents. If the matter or object to be expedited "*in forma Bullae*" is a very important one, such as the confirmation of a bishop, the erection or division of a diocese, or a solemn act of the R. Pontiff, the leaden seal hanging on a silken cord is appended. If, however, the Bull contains matter of less importance, *v. g.,*

4 Cf. Bresslau, *Handbuch der Urkundenlehre,* 1889, Vol. 1 (only one vol. published), p. 67 ff.; also Mabillon, *De Re Diplomatica,* Paris, 1681.

5 The original meaning of *bulla* is gem (precious ornament), then seal, from which it is transferred to the document provided with a seal, cf. *Thesaurus Linguae Lat.,* 1906, II, p. 2241 f., Du Cange, *Glossarium,* II, p. 1339.

dispositions regarding minor benefices or matrimonial dispensations, the document has a seal of red wax with the images of SS. Peter and Paul, and around them the name of the reigning Pontiff.[6] The opening words are: " [*Benedictus XV*] *Episcopus Servus Servorum Dei.*" [7] A special kind of Bull are the "*Bullae dimidiatae*," which are issued between the election and coronation of a Pope, and bear only the image of the two Apostles, whilst the reverse side of the seal is blank.[8]

β) *Brevia*, or Briefs, which have grown out of the letters closed with wax, are issued in the *Secretaria Brevium*, and generally concern minor affairs (*negotia non gravia*), although, at times, in order to save expenses, Briefs are issued regarding matters which would really require a Bull, *v. g.*, the erection of *Abbatiae Nullius*. They begin with the name of the Pontiff, thus: "*Benedictus Papa XV*," and end with the words: "*Sub annulo piscatoris.*"

" Motu Proprio's " and Rescripts have no special form.

We may add that the *Bullae* are now no longer written in Gothic but in the usual Latin letters, on parchment.[9]

b) Concerning their *juridical* value, it must be noticed that papal documents are variously styled: a) *Constitutions*, named after the ancient imperial constitutions, are Apostolic letters referring to important matters which concern the universal, or at least the entire Western Church. They may also be called, not improperly, *En-*

6 *Acta Leonis XIII*, 1881, t. I, p. 184 f.

7 This title dates back to the pontificate of St. Gregory the Great (590-604), and is of monastic origin, the monks calling themselves " servants of God," and this Pope, to reprove the arrogance of the Byzantine patriarch, styled himself "Servant of the servants of God."

8 Cf. *Cironii Observationes*, ed. Riegger, 1761, p. 5.

9 Thus ordained by Leo XIII, Dec. 29, 1878; cfr. *Archiv für kath. Kirchenrecht*, Vol. 41, p. 399; Aichner, *Compendium Juris Ecclesiastici*, § 10.

cyclical letters, though these generally refer to the persons addressed (viz.: the hierarchy) and contain less juridical matter (*v. g.*, " Rerum novarum," of Leo XIII, 1891).

β) *Decrees;* or *decretals*, to which belong those letters issued " Motu proprio " and " ad instantiam " (rescripts), broadly speaking, touch upon particular affairs and contain favors and privileges or answers to questions proposed by private individuals. It must, however, be added that " Motu proprio " does not exclude insistence or a request from interested parties.

ARTICLE 3

THE CANONS OF COUNCILS

Councils, as history testifies, were generally called at times when a crisis threatened the Church at large, or at least a considerable portion thereof. Although the first four general councils were convoked by the emperors, the " Bishop of old Rome " was represented by legates, and the decrees adopted were acknowledged by the universal Church. St. Gregory the Great speaks of those four councils as of four gospels.[10] Besides these imposing assemblies there were held provincial councils, *v. g.*, at Antioch, Ancyra, Sardis, which also enjoyed great authority. Still a distinction was always made between universal and particular synods; the canons of the former were received by all, whilst those of the latter had only local force, except when they were inserted in an authentic collection of Canon Laws. No authentic collection of conciliary decrees as such exists. Of general Councils, two were held at Nicaea in Bythinia (325, 787),

10 *Registrum Greg.*, P. I, 24, ed. Ewald-Hartmann (*M. G.*), 1891, I, 36 (this is a model *epistola synodica*).

four at Constantinople (381, 553, 680, and 869), one at Ephesus (431) and Chalcedon (451), four at the Lateran (1123, 1139, 1179, 1215), two at Lyons (1245, 1274), one at Vienne (1311–13), one at Constance (1414–18), one at Basel-Ferrara-Florence (1431–45), one at Trent (1545–63), and one at the Vatican.

ARTICLE 4

THE UNWRITTEN LAW

A certain amount of traditional law is in vogue everywhere. It is the living spirit of the people's judgment, or "common sense." The Church, too, has her *traditions*, which testify to the observance of discipline, although there may be no corresponding law. Thus the celebration of the Sunday instead of the Jewish Sabbath[11] is called a divine tradition. Human traditions are, *e. g.*, that which causes Easter to be celebrated on a certain day and the existence of minor orders.

Besides, there are *writings* of *ecclesiastical authors* which prove the existence of certain customs in ancient times. These, however, if not embodied in an authentic collection, have merely historical value.

Leaving traditions aside as being now defined and to a great extent determined, Canon Law is more especially interested in *custom*, which shall be treated in the Commentary proper.

11 C. 5, Dist. 11.

CHAPTER IV

HISTORY OF THE SOURCES AND LITERATURE OF CANON LAW

The chief authorities to be consulted are:

BALLERINI, Peter and Jerome, in their ed. of the *Opera Leonis M.*, t. 3 (Migne, *Pat. Lat.*, t. 56) ;

P. COUSTANT, O.S.B., *Epistolae Rom. Pontificum*, Parisiis, 1721, Praef. ;

F. LAURIN, *Introductio in Corpus Juris Can.*, Friburgi, 1889 ;

F. MAASSEN, *Geschichte der Quellen u. der Literatur des Canonischen Rechts*, Gratz, 1870 (Vol. 1, the only one published) ;

J. F. SCHULTE, *Geschichte der Quellen u. Literatur des Canonischen Rechts von Gratian bis auf die Gegenwart*, 1875, 3 vols. ;

AUG. THEINER, *Disquisitiones Criticae*, 1836.

The critical and historical method of treating the sources of Canon Law began with Humanism, or, more properly, with Nicholas of Cusa (Cusanus, + 1464). That the Pseudo-Isidorian Collection should be first attacked was natural. But this was but a beginning. Much remained to be done in regard to papal letters and conciliary decrees. A great deal had been achieved by the Spaniard Antonius Augustinus, in the sixteenth century, but his work was left incomplete. More elaborate were the critical labors of the brothers Peter and Jerome Ballerini, who deserve a distinguished place in canonistic literature.   The names of Maassen and Schulte also are favorably known in this line of studies.

We can give only a brief historical sketch of the collections made according to the various epochs which Canon Law traversed.

SECTION 1

FIRST PERIOD (TO ABOUT 1150)

Some disciplinary regulations are to be found in the so-called "*Constitutiones Apostolorum*," a fifth-century collection, made up of the "Doctrina XII Apostolorum," "Didascalia Apostolorum," and "Canones Ecclesiastici Apostolorum," to which were added the "Canones Hippolyti."[1] This collection, made by an anonymous writer imbued with heretical tendencies, contains some traditional customs concerning episcopal elections, ordination and qualities of aspirants to the priesthood, minor orders, etc. But it cannot properly be termed a source of Canon Law.

A collection of conciliar canons must have existed at the time of the Council of Chalcedon (451). Most probably this collection contained the enactments of "*Seven Councils,*" *viz.*: those of Nice, Ancyra, Neo-Cæsarea, Gangræ, Antioch, Laodicæa, and Constantinople. To these were added later the canons of the councils of Ephesus, Chalcedon and Sardis (343), and the combined collection was eventually called *Collectio Decem Conciliorum.*[2] To this were prefixed the "Canones Apostolorum," 85 in number, which were received by the Trullan Synod held in the year 691–692 and are still

---

[1] Cfr. Funk, *Didascalia et Constitutiones*, 1906; O. Bardenhewer, *Geschichte der altchristlichen Literatur*, 1903, Vol. 2, pp. 69, 255 ff.; Bardenhewer-Shahan, *Patrology*, 1908, pp. 349 ff.

[2] Maassen, *op. cit.*, pp. 126 ff.; P. Coustant, *op. cit.*, pp. LVIII.

acknowledged in the Eastern Church as "*Codex Ecclesiae Orientalis.*"[3]

Whilst these collections were chronological, the later ones were *systematic,* beginning with one by an unknown author and another by Joannes Scholasticus (c. 550), distributed into 50 titles.

Another species of systematic collections were those styled "*Nomocanones,*" containing, as the name implies, both civil (νόμος) and ecclesiastical (κάνων) laws. Several such collections were made in the sixth and seventh centuries and one of them was revised by Photius (c. 883).[4] This caesaro-papistic collection was based on the still acknowledged principle of the Oriental Church that " in illis quae canones non determinarunt, debemus sequi leges civiles."[5]

ARTICLE 1

OCCIDENTAL COLLECTIONS

The Greek collections mentioned above found their way into the Latin Church as early as the close of the fifth century, when a translation of the Greek canons was made and spread in Italy and Spain. In this latter country the spread of the Latin translation of the Eastern Councils was due especially to Isidore of Seville, and hence it goes by the name of *Isidoriana,* whilst the Latin translation used in Italy was called "*Prisca.*"[6]

In the latter country, most probably in Rome, a

3 Milasch-Pessič, *Kirchenrecht der abendländischen Kirche,* 1905, pp. 81 ff.

4 V. Scherer, *l. c.,* I, 197.

5 Cfr. *Syntagma Atheniense,* I, 68 (Milasch, *l. c.,* p. 50).

6 It was thus called from the preface of the Dionysian version, "priscae translationis." Cfr. *Voelli et Justelli Bibliotheca Juris Can.,* Paris, 1661, t. 1, p. 101; Maassen, *l. c.,* pp. 87 ff; Ballerini (Migne, 56, col. 83 f.).

Scythian monk, *Dionysius Exiguus* (Denys the Little,
+ before 555), made a translation of the Greek canons,
213 in number, to which he added fifty " Canones Apostolorum " and 138 canons of African councils. This
collection was increased by the " Decretales SS. Pontificum " issued from the time of Siricius (384–94) to the
pontificate of Anastasius (+ 498), 197 in number. A
copy of this double collection of conciliar canons and
papal decrees, with some additional decretals, was do-
nated by Pope Hadrian I to Charlemagne in 774, and
subsequently called *Dionysio-Hadriana*. It enjoyed
great authority in Italy, Gaul, Africa, Spain, and England.[7]

In *Africa* a collection of the decrees of councils held
from 397 onward was made at an early date and con-
densed into the " *Breviatio Canonum* " of Fulgentius
Furandus towards the middle of the sixth century. A
systematic handbook destined for school use was the
work entitled " Concordia Canonum " of Cresconius,
published in the year 690.[8]

Of *Gallic* origin are the so-called "*Statuta Ecclesiae
Antiqua*" of the sixth century.[9] Another collection of
French descent is that named from its editor Paschase
Quesnel, *Quesnelliana*, and the one published by d'Achery,
O.S.B. (+ 1685), called *Dacheriana*.[10] The latter au-
thor also edited a collection of penitential canons which
goes by the same name, but was originally called " Collec-
tio Canonum."

Spain had the *Isidoriana*, which through the magic
name of St. Isidore (+ 636) gained great authority, and

[7] Maassen, *l. c.*, pp. 444 ff.; pp.
965 ff.; Migne, *l. c.*, 195 f.

[8] Mabillon, *Iter Italicum*, 1724,
II; ed. Th. Sickel, 1889.

[9] Migne, 56, 282; 273 f.; Maassen,
l. c., 79 f.; 806 ff.

[10] Ballerini, *l. c.* (Migne, 53,
106 f.); Maassen, *l. c.*, 382 f.

was twice revised between 589 A. D. and the close of the seventh century; and a collection made by, or published under the name of, Martin of Braga, and circulated as *"Capitula Martini."* [11]

Besides these collections of Canon Law proper, the *Penitential Books,* published especially in Ireland, England and France, enjoyed great esteem. [12]

For the *jus liturgicum* the *Sacramentaria* [13] and *Ordines Romani* [14] are of great importance. For the chancery of the Roman Curia, its style and methods of expedition, the *" Liber Diurnus "* is invaluable.

ARTICLE 2

SPURIOUS COLLECTIONS OF THE NINTH CENTURY

The ninth century was rife with fabrications, not only in hagiography, but also in Canon Law. To this category belongs a collection named *Continuatio ad Capitularia Regum Francorum,* which the Levite Benedict of Mayence professes to have taken from the archives of that Church and compiled at the request of Bishop Hatto (825-47). It contains genuine canons and decrees side by side with spurious ones manufactured by Benedict. [15] Not much different in character and style are the *Capitula Angilramni.* Both this and the former collections originated in northeastern France. [16]

11 Migne, 141 f.; 309; Maassen, 436 f.; 536 ff.; 848 ff.

12 Migne, 53, 218; Maassen, 802 ff.; 677 ff.

13 Cfr. Wasserschleben, *Die Bussordnungen der abendländischen Kirche,* 1851; Schmitz, *Die Bussbücher,* 1883.

14 Probst, *Die ältesten röm. Sacramentarien,* 1892.

15 Cfr. *Monumenta Germaniae Historica, Leges,* II, 2, 39-158.

16 Cfr. Hinschius, *Decretales Pseudo-Isidorianae et Capitula Angilramni,* 1863, Praef., CXCIII ff.; CCXXX, p. 757.

The Pseudo-Isidorian Decretals

This collection has, since the fifteenth century, claimed the attention of critics. That it contained considerable fraudulent matter was perceived by the famous humanist, Cardinal Nicholas of Cusa,[17] and has since been acknowledged by most " Romanists," although some later writers, like Torres, Malvasia, and Cardinal d'Aguirre, defended its genuineness.

1. *Contents.* The collection consists of a preface and three parts. The *Præfatio* contains the foreword of pseudo-Isidore (*Mercator* or *Peccator*), a spurious letter of Aurelius of Carthage to Pope Damasus with the latter's equally spurious reply, and the " Ordo de Celebrando Concilio."

Part I contains 50 *Canones Apostolorum* and *decretals* of Popes from Clement I to Melchiades (+ 314) — the latter, with the exception of the Clementine letters, all manufactured by " Mercator." [18]

Part II is made up of (a) *De Primitiva Ecclesia*, (b) *Exemplar Constituti Constantini*, and (c) *Canons of Councils* from the Nicene to the second of Spain, partly in the form of the *Hispana*, partly in that of the *Quesnelliana*.[19]

Part III exhibits some excerpts from Pope Silvester and a number of genuine *decretals* from Mark (+ 336) to Gregory II (715-31) in the form of the *Hispana*.[20] The number of apocryphal decretals is about 46 and that of the chapters which the author himself compiled about 104.[21]

17 *Concordantia Catholica*, III, 2; **ff.**
Ballerini (Migne, 56, 210).
18 Hinschius, *l. c.*, p. LXX.
19 Hinschius, *l. c.*, pp. LXXXIII
20 Hinschius, LXXXIX.
21 Cfr. Coustant, *l. c.*, CXXVI; Hinschius, CVIII.

2. *Author* and *Time of Composition*. It is commonly held that the birth-place of these pseudo-decretals must be sought, not in Rome (as Eichhorn and Theiner claimed), but in the western part of France. The exact place still forms a matter of controversy. While some (*v. g.* Hinschius [22] and von Scherer [23]) regard the diocese of Rheims as the home of the fraudulent compiler, others (especially Fournier [24]) assign him to the province of Tours and in particular to Le Mans.

As to the *time* of compilation there is no great divergency of opinion, for it is generally set between 847 and 853.[25]

3. *Purpose of the Compiler*. It is scarcely credible that the author had for his sole purpose the aggrandizement and defense of the Apostolic See,[26] or that of the bishops of Gaul or any particular part of it.[27] He says in the preface that he desired to gather the scattered canons into one volume. However, this was not his only purpose, otherwise his fabrications would have been superfluous. There can be no doubt that the compiler had still another end in view. This was, as Fournier [28] and others set forth, a twofold one: (a) to protect the authority of the bishops and clergy against encroachments of the potentates and lay-power at large, and (b) to secure the authority of the Roman Pontiff over particular synods, and to defend the hierarchy in all its degrees. Concerning the first point the emphasis laid on immunity is most notable. As to the other point it may be noticed

22 Pseudo-Decretals, Pref., CCXI.

23 *Handbuch des Kirchenrechts*, 1887, I, 222 f.

24 *Les Fausses Décrétals*, in Re-vue d'Histoire Éccl., 1906, 784.

25 Hinschius, *l. c.*, p. CCI.

26 Ballerini (Migne, 53, 246).

27 Hinschius, *l. c.*, CCXIII f.

28 *Revue. d'Hist. Éccl.*, 1906, p. 548.

that the Apostolic See was not in need of apocryphal documents to assert its rights.[29]

4. *Influence of the Collection.* It has frequently been said that Pseudo-Isidore ushered in an entirely new discipline. If this were true, only a solemn anathema on that fraudulent writer could repair the damage done to Canon Law. However, we must beware of both extremes — overrating the influence exercised by this collection as well as minimizing it unduly. A little distinction may be helpful in determining its true influence.

The *material* sway it exerted we see in the greater dependence of bishops and provinces on the Holy See — more centralisation — and in the outspoken tendency of the compiler to accentuate what we comprise by the term "immunity," and by extending the matrimonial degrees, which was then unheard of.

The *formal* influence consisted in the precision and divulgation of laws which, though already existing, were not yet accurately determined, *v. g.*, concerning the confirmation and deposition of bishops, appeals, immunity. It cannot be denied that this fraud rendered a bad service to Canon Law, bringing it into discredit and evil repute for a time.[30]

In *Germany* two collections were widely known and made use of, to which may be added a third. They are:

a) Regino of Prüm's "*De Synodalibus Causis et Disciplinis Ecclesiasticis,*" which was made between 906 and 915, in which latter year Abbot Regino died.[31]

---

29 Ballerini (Migne, 56, 246).

30 Von Scherer, *l. c.*, I, 227; Coustant, *l. c.*, Praef., CXXVII. An excellent monograph in English, by a Protestant lawyer, is now available in *The False Decretals*, by E. H. Davenport, Oxford, 1916.

31 Cfr. Ballerini (Migne, 56, 319); Regino's collection was published in Migne, 132, 17 f. and by Wasserschleben, 1840.

. b) More renowned is the *"Decretum Burchardi."* Burchard was Bishop of Worms, and composed his collection for practical purposes, especially for the visitation of his diocese. It consists of twenty books, the nineteenth of which is called " Corrector sive Medicus " and treats of penitential discipline. Burchard's chief sources were the " Collectio Anselmo Dicata," whose arrangement he adopted, and Regino's collection. Besides, he quoted many false decretals (about 173 in number), and invented new ones (about 59). He also changed or mutilated the inscriptions of titles and chapters.[82] But despite all these shortcomings the work found a ready reception, not only in Germany, but also in Italy, where Gratian introduced it into his Decretum [83] as " Brocardicae."

c) Belonging to the " Gregorian " group is the " *Capitulare* " or " *Breviarium Hattonis,*" composed about 1080.[84]

ARTICLE 3

COLLECTIONS OF THE TENTH AND ELEVENTH CENTURIES

The Pseudo-Isidorian Decretals were followed by other collections, more or less spurious, not only in France, but in Italy and Germany as well. The age was prolific in forgeries.

1. In *Italy* there was one published which is not as yet printed, although it would, according to our view, based upon inspection of the original MSS.,[85] deserve

82 Cfr. Fournier, *Études Critiques.*
83 See Friedberg, *Decretum Magistri Gratiani,* Leipsic, 1879, pp. XLV ff.
84 Edited by Mai, *Nova Biblio-*
theca Patrum, VII, P. III, 1-76; v. Scherer, *l. c.,* I, 240.
85 Contained in the Cod. Paris. 15392, Cod. Mutinens.; besides in the Palat. Vat. 580 and 581, which

more attention.   This, the *"Collectio Anselmo Dicata,"* was made towards the end of the ninth century.

The investiture controversy brought forth some collections which are all imbued with the spirit of Gregory VII and therefore called *"Collectiones Gregorianae."* To this group belong:

a) The *Collectio Anselmi Lucani* (Anselm of Lucca, + 1086);

b) The *"Collectio Canonum Cardinalis Deusdedit,"* dedicated to Pope Victor III (1086-87); [36]

c) The *"Decretales Bonizonis,"* composed soon after 1089;

d) The *"Polycarpus"* of Cardinal Gregory, issued soon after the death of Pope Calixt II (+ 1124).

The Vatican Library furthermore contains some interesting MSS. pertaining to collections of that period, which await publication. [37]

3. In *France* some notable special treatises were published, *e. g.*, Hincmar of Rheims' *"De Divortio Lothari Regis,"* [38] and Jonas of Orleans' (+ 843) *"De Laicali et Institutione Regali."* [39]   *Collections* proper are:

a) The *"Canones Domni Abbonis"* of Fleury (+ 1004), dedicated to King Hugh and his son Robert, a collection of genuine canons and papal decretals, also containing *Capitularia Regum Francorum* and *Novellae.* [40]

b) A *"Compilatio Juris Canonici"* of about the

---

are written in the Carolingian minuscules. This Anselm, to whom it is dedicated, was Archbishop of Milan, 883-97; cfr. Ballerini (Migne, 56, 315 ff.), Coustant, *l. c.*, Praef., CXXVI; Fournier, *Études Critiques sur le Décret de Burchard de Worms*, 1910, p. 10.

[36] Published by Martinucci, 1869, and by Wolf von Glanvell, 1905.
[37] Cod. 1339 in 5 books; Cod. 1346 in 7 books, more or less dependent on Pseudo-Isidore.
[38] Migne, *Pat. Lat.*, 125, 623 ff.
[39] Migne, *l. c.*, 106, 121 ff.
[40] Ballerini (Migne, 56, 320, 139, 473 ff.).

same date, treating of the reception of heretics and some of the sources of Canon Law.[41]

c) The *"Decretum Ivonis Carnotensis"* (+ 1117), which consists of seventeen books, and the same author's *"Panormia"* in eight parts. The former is a rich collection not only of canonical matter but also of theological lore, *e. g.*, on baptism, confirmation and the Holy Eucharist. The "Panormia" was said to be the compilation made from Ivo's Decretum by the Catalonian Hugo, but it is probably Ivo's work.[42]

d) A *"Collectio Trium Partium,"* divided into 29 titles, was made from Ivo's work soon after his death.[43] Then there is the work of *Alger* of *Liège* "De misericordia et justitia," c. 1121, consisting of three parts.[44]

In *Spain* a collection of 15 books appeared shortly after the Pontificate of Urban II (1088–1109).[45]

---

41 V. Scherer, I, 238.

42 Theiner, *l. c.*, pp. 162 f.; Migne, 56, 104.

43 Theiner, *l. c.*, pp. 154 ff.

44 Migne, 180, 857 ff.; v. Scherer I, 242.

45 Ballerini (Migne, 56, 352 f.).

SECTION 2

This epoch is distinguished by two prominent characteristics. Canon Law becomes independent of theology as such and is cultivated as a *science* proper. The "Magister" ushers in that period, so glorious for canonical lore and resplendent with names immortal. The appearance of standard or *authentic collections* sheds lustre on Canon Law, which now grows into Pontifical Law and irradiates immediately from St. Peter's Chair. These authentic collections are now, first of all, to be considered. It is necessary, however, to premise a few words on the famous *Decretum Gratiani.*

ARTICLE 1

THE DECRETUM MAGISTRI GRATIANI

1. AUTHOR AND NAME.—As the glossators testify, the author of the famous Decree is *Gratian,* who lived and taught as a member of the monastery of SS. Felix and Nabor at Bologna. It is most probable that this monastery then belonged to the Camaldulese. Of Gratian's career we know nothing, except that he died before A. D. 1160.[1]

There is historical evidence that the "Magister," as he was called, had entitled his work "*Concordia Discordan-*

---

1 Cfr. Maurus Sarti, O. Cam., *De Claris Archigymnasii Bononiensis Professoribus,* 1769-72; Schulte, *Quellen,* 1875, Vol. I, pp. 46 f.; Laurin, *l. c.,* p. 10.

tium Canonum." [2]   His purpose, according to his disciple,
the famous Magister Rolandus (later Alexander III),[3]
was to make apparently contradictory canons agree
and to remove latent divergencies. However, already
towards the end of the twelfth century, the collection
was commonly called *Decretum Magistri Gratiani,* although it was also cited by the names " Codex," " Corpus," or " Liber Decretorum," or simply, " Corpus Juris
Canonici." [4]

2. DIVISION.—The threefold general division was made
by Gratian himself,— *De Personis, De Causis, De Sacramentis.*[5]

Part I consists of 101 distinctions, divided into canons,
— but not by Gratian.   It contains a treatise on the principles of Canon Law and a long treatise " *De Electione
et Ordinatione Clericorum.*"

Part II was divided by Gratian himself into 36 *Causae,*
and each causa into *Quæstiones,* which, in their turn, were
subdivided into *Canones.*   The first ten *Causae* might
be inscribed " *De Judiciis*"; *Causae* 11-20, " *De Bonis
Ecclesiasticis et Regularibus.*"   *Causae* 21–26 treat of
benefices and privileges, *Causae* 27–36, of marriage.

Causa 33, Quaestio III, contains the " *Tractatus de
Poenitentia,*" which Gratian inserted here, but did not
himself divide into seven *Distinctiones,* as we now have
it.

Part III was inscribed, " *Liber de Sacramentis,*" for
which title Paucapalea substituted " *De Consecratione.*"
It is divided into five distinctions.[6]

3. MODE OF ALLEGING.—A canonist will never quote,

2 Friedberg, *Decretum Magistri
Gratiani,* 1879, Prol., X.
3 *Summa Magistri Rolandi,* ed.
Thaner, 1874, p. 4.

4 Laurin, *Introductio,* p. 25.
5 Cfr. Schulte, *Quellen,* I, 50 ff.
6 *Ibid.,* I, 50 ff.

e. g., "*in Decreto Gratiani,*" but follow the usual mode of citing the decree:

Part I: *c. i, D. i,* which would read: Canon first, Distinction first. Sometimes we find the initial words only quoted, *e. g.,* "*Si quis apostolicae,*" LXXIX, which is Can. 1, Dist. 79. Of course, in that case the index must be consulted, which now takes the place of memory, on which the law-students of former times had to rely.

Part II has the distinctive sign C (Causae, written with a capital C), taking the middle between canons and questions, thus: *c. 29, C. 17, q. 4,* or again with the initial words of the canon: "*Si quis suadente diabolo,*" which is the canon quoted in number and abbreviated letters. *De Poenitentia:* c. i, Dist. 5 de Poenit. which reads: canon 1, Distinction 5, with the characteristic sign, "*De Poenit.*" We must draw attention to the fact that two of the *Causae* exhibit a transposition of questions; in *Causa 2, quaestio* 5 is placed immediately after 3; and in *Causa* 16, *quaestio* 5 directly follows 3.[7]

Part III: *c. 16, Dist. 5 de consecr(atione),* which signifies canon 16, Distinction 5 *de consecratione;* or again with the beginning words: "*Quadragesima summae*" *de consecr.*

Note that older canonists simply quote "*in Decretis*" with the initial words of the canons, and if the text does not fully cover the proof, they say "*arg*" (*argumentum*).[8]

4. RUBRICAE, DICTA GRATIANI, PALEAE.—To show the author's method it suffices to point out the brief summaries which precede almost every canon or authority alleged by the "Magister." These summaries are placed at the head in red (ruber) ink and hence called *rubricae.*[9]

---

7 Laurin, *l. c.,* p. 7 (thus also in Friedberg's edition).

8 *Id.,* pp. 9 f.

9 Cfr. Schulte, *l. c.,* I, 54.

Furthermore, the Master employed at times some longer expositions, which were either to prove his view on certain canons or a deduction from the authorities alleged. These elucidations were styled *paragraphi* or *d:cta Gratiani.* They are to be found either before or after a *distinctio* or *causa* or *quaestio*, and savor of the scholastic disputation.[10] They were intended to remove contradictions between different canons by pointing out that one canon formed the rule, whereas the other was an exception, or that one contained a precept, whereas the other was only a counsel; one emanated from a higher, the other from some inferior authority; one was given for the universal Church, whereas the other referred to a particular province, etc.[11]

The *Decretum*, as now published, contains many *additions* which are not the work of Gratian. It is certain that the Master's disciple, Paucapalea, added some decretals, wherefore all the additions were called *paleae.*[12] Their number is not quite certain, perhaps they form 166 out of the 3848 chapters of which the *Decretum* consists.[13]

5. SOURCES AND AUTHORITY.—(1) The sources are either directly or indirectly taken from their collections and collectors. The *direct* sources are 17 apostolic canons, apocryphal as well as genuine decretals from Pseudo-Isidore, the writings of the Fathers, four chapters from St. Benedict's Rule, and Roman, Visigothic and Frankish civil laws.

Indirect sources were those of the collections: Anselmo dicata, Regino, Burchard, Luccani, Deusdedit, Polycarp,

---

10 *Ib.,* 55 ff. A famous *"dictum Gratiani"* is that ad c. 16, C. 25, q. 1, on the nature of privileges.

11 Schulte, *l. c.,* I, 60; v. Scherer, *l. c.,* I, 243.

12 Another explanation, *viz.* that of " straw " (*palea*), is given by Huguccio, ad c. 51, C. 27, q. 2.

13 Friedberg, *l. c.,* Proleg., p. XIV; Schulte, *l. c.,* I, 56 ff.

Ivo, Algerius.[14] But the lack of critical genius of his age is also noticeable in Gratians' work.

(2) The reception given to the *Decretum* is almost incredible in our critical time. It was called "*opus aureum*" or "*divinum decretorum opus.*"[15] There seems to be a reason for the applause with which the Magister's work was hailed: on account of the rich materials he had gathered and the scientific method he had adopted, especially in his "*dicta*" and general arrangement, the Decree soon made other collections superfluous and was generally used in schools and courts.[16]

In spite of all this veneration, however, the *Decretum Gratiani* has *never* been considered or declared an *authentic collection*. It was made by private authority and remained such. Hence its authority is neither more nor less than the sources laid under contribution are worth. A decree made by a universal council (*consideratis considerandis*) has the value of a universal law; a canon adopted by a particular council receives no additional force by being inserted in the Decree beyond that which it had before Gratian, etc. Hence each source must be examined independently as to its origin, authenticity, and authority.

At the same time it must be remembered that the Decree, on account of its popularity and the influence it exerted on teachers and judges, paved the way for other collections, which were no longer of merely private authority.

6. Time and Editions.—When Gratian composed his *Decretum* is a matter of controversy. We do not be-

14 Friedberg, *l. c.*, pp. XIX ff.; p. XLII.

15 Cfr. Berardi, *Gratiani Canones Genuini*, 1783, I; Sarti, *l. c.*, 1, 247;

Laurin, *l. c.*, pp. 44 f.

16 Sarti, *l. c.*, I, 247; Berardi, *l. c.*, Praef., XXVIII; Schulte, *l. c.*, I, 329.

lieve that intrinsic reasons will ever be found to clearly determine the time of its birth. What has been urged [17] in favor of an earlier than the usually accepted date, is not solidly proved nor free from bias. Extrinsic reasons rather favor 1150–1151 as the probable year of publication. The glossa of Joannes Teutonicus ad c. 31, C. 3, q. 6 and an old MS. state these two years, respectively.[18]

In the course of centuries the *Decretum* was often copied, sometimes with and sometimes without *glossae*, and the faithful rendering of the original text depended on the care of the copyists. Mistakes and corrections were already noticed by St. Antoninus (+ 1459) and they increased after the art of printing had been invented. Antony de Mouchy, in the edition of 1547, and Antony Conte, in the Paris edition of 1556 and the Antwerp edition of 1570, drew attention to spurious decretals. The *Correctores Romani* endeavored to eliminate some palpable errors and to render the text more intelligible. In 1580 and 1582 appeared a so-called official but not authentic text.[19] Henceforward the *Decretum* was reprinted by private savants, generally in connection with the "*Corpus Juris Canonici*." [20]

APPENDICES AND COMPILATIONS.—Soon after the publication of the Decree some decretals were added to it or separately published, e. g., the "*Appendix Concilii Lateranensis*," the "*Collectio Bambergensis*," the "*Collectio Lipsiensis*," the "*Decretales Alexandri III.*" [21]

---

[17] The formula "*salvâ sedis apostolicae auctoritate*" has been alleged by Theiner and Schulte to prove 1139 as the year of divulgation.

[18] The codex reads: "*Decretum Gratiani, monachi, Felicis Bononiensis, Ord. S. Benedicti completum in dicto monasterio anno Dmi. MCLI,*

tempore Eugenii tertii;" Laurin, *l. c.*, p. 34.

[19] Theiner, *l. c.*, app., p. 3; Friedberg, Prolog., LXXV ff.

[20] Cfr. below on the whole C. J. C.

[21] Cfr. Theiner, *l. c.*, p. 4 ff.; Schulte, *l. c.*, I, 77 ff.

Of greater importance than these were the five so-called *Compilationes, viz.*:

a) *Compilatio I Bernardi Papiensis*, entitled by the author "Breviarium Extravagantium," issued between 1187 and 1191, divided into 5 books with titles and chapters according to the famous verse, "*iudex, judicium, clerus, connubia, crimen.*"

b) *Compilatio II*, by John of Wales (Joannes Walensis), published before 1200. Neither of these compilations is *authentic*, whereas the folowing three must be considered authentic:

c) *Compilatio III*, made at the request of Innocent III by Petrus Collavicinus or Beneventanus (1210).

d) *Compilatio IV*, perhaps made by Innocent III himself, and consequently before or about 1216, although published only in 1217.

e) *Compilatio V*, made and promulgated under the auspices of Honorius III, 1226.[22] These three collections were alleged in schools and courts in the same manner as the Decretals.

ARTICLE 2

DECRETALES GREGORII IX (1234)

1. NAME.—By a Bull dated Sept. 5th, 1234, Gregory IX promulgated a collection of "Constitutions and Decretals," to which he himself, referring to the five preceding, attributed the name "*compilatio.*" It was soon called "*nova*" (*scil. compilatio*) as well as "*Liber Extravagantium*" (*scil. extra Decretum*) and added to the five other compilations. However, the name "Decre-

22 Cfr. Theiner, *l. c.*, pp. 1 ff.; Schulte, *l. c.*, I, 80 ff.; Laurin, *l. c.*, 97 ff.; Friedberg, *Quinque Compila-* *tiones Antiquae*, 1882; v. Scherer, I, 247, 31.

tales " became more usual and finally exclusive,[23] and is now constantly employed.

The *reason* for this collection is stated in the Bull " Rex pacificus " as follows: Some decretals, on account of their length and resemblance to each other, appeared to cause confusion and uncertainty in the schools as well as courts, and to remedy this evil, the present collection is issued as an *authentic* one, to be employed in schools and ecclesiastic courts *exclusively* of all others. This meant that (a) the former five compilations were henceforward destitute of juridical value, and therefore could not be alleged as law-texts by the ecclesiastical judges; (b) each and every chapter in its dispositive part, no matter what its source or authority, was to have full juridical value as a law-text; (c) the collection was to be considered *the* Code of Law for the universal (Latin) Church, to the exclusion of all others of a general character. But this collection did not abrogate either the *Decretum Gratiani* or existing particular laws and customs, nor did it prevent the publication of later codes.[24]

2. COMPILER AND MATTER.—As the Bull " Rex pacificus " tells us, the Pope commissioned his chaplain and confessor, Bl. Raymund de Peñaforte (+ 1275), to make this compilation, and he accomplished his task within the space of four years, so that the collection could be published in 1234.

The *material* was gathered from Holy Scripture, from the canons of particular as well as universal councils, and from papal decretals. A few are taken from the civil laws. Most of the Decretals, with the exception of those of Innocent III and Gregory IX, were copied from the " five compilations." There are 1971 chapters, of which

23 Friedberg, *Corpus Juris Can.*, II, Proleg., p. X.   24 Laurin, *l. c.*, pp. 141 ff.; v. Scherer, I, 251 f.

1766 are borrowed from the compilations mentioned.

3. ORDER AND MODE OF QUOTING.—The whole collection is divided into five *books* according to the well-known verse quoted above (p. 36), each book into *titles*, and each title into *chapters*. Each title has an inscription, and the chapters are generally preceded by *rubrics* or brief summaries, which, however, are of purely private authority, whereas the *titles*, whenever their words exhibit a complete meaning (*e. g.*, " *Ne sede vacante aliquid innovetur*," III, 9) have legal value. When the decretals appeared too long, Raymund cut off the *arenga*, or *narratio*, retaining only the dispositive part. The cut-off parts ("*partes decisae*") were marked "*et infra*." The modern way of *quoting* these decretals is: *c. 4, X, I, 4*, *i. e.*, chapter 4, liber extravangantium (viz. extra or outside the Decretum Gratiani and the five compilations), book first, title fourth. Sometimes the beginning of the chapter is quoted with " extra " and the inscription of the title, v. g., *De Consuetudine*.

ARTICLE 3

DECRETALES BONIFACII VIII (1298)

From the time of Gregory IX the Roman Pontiffs developed much legislative activity. Thus Innocent IV (Fiesco), a canonist of merit, issued various Decretals, which he himself collected and divided into 28 titles with 42 chapters. Another collection was sent by the same Pope to the famous University of Bologna, in 1253.[25] Alexander IV, Clement IV, and Urban IV also issued Decretals, which were sometimes simply added to Greg-

---

[25] Theiner, *l. c.*, p. 66; Schulte, *Quellen*, II, 30 ff.; Laurin, *l. c.*, pp. 166 ff.

ory's collection, sometimes remained " x," as *Novellae*.[26]
These motley decretals caused some uncertainty.   Where-
upon three dignitaries, William, Archbishop of Embruns,
Berengarius, Bishop of Beziers, and Richard of Siena,
Vice-chancellor S.R.E., were ordered by the Pope to
" revise " the Decretals, and after revision, to send them
to the universities of Bologna and Paris.   This was done
in 1298, and the collection thus made at the request of
Boniface VIII was added to the existing Decretals of
Gregory IX as a continuation to the same, and therefore
called "*Liber Sextus.*"   So we read in the Bull " Sacrosanctae," March 3, 1298.[27]

I. MATTER AND ARRANGEMENT.—The three above-
named compilers took their materials from the canons
of the first and second Councils of Lyons (1245, 1274)
and from the Decretals of Gregory and his successors up
to Martin IV and Boniface VIII.   The Decretals of the
latter form 229 chapters.   The compilers made use of the
preceding compilations and added the eighty-eight " *Regulae Juris,*" taken from Dinus of Mugello (de Rossoni-
bus).[28]

The title headings were taken from Gregory's, also the
rubrics as well as the inscriptions of the single chapters.
The latter, however, were often abridged, sometimes
changed, and sometimes even wrongly quoted.   The
" *partes decisae* " were no longer marked " *et infra,*" but
simply " cut off."   On the whole this collection is not
as faithful and precise a rendering of the original text of
the Decretals as one might have expected from Boniface
VIII, but it has the character of a juridical code.   Al-

26 Schulte, *l. c.*, pp. 31 f.; Laurin,
l. c., pp. 171 ff.
27 Friedberg, *Corpus Juris Can.*,
II, 933 f.

28 Sarti, *l. c.*, I, 234 ff.; v.
Scherer, *l. c.*, I, 252; Laurin, *l. c.*,
177.

though called "*Liber Sextus*" and intended, as it were, to be a continuation of the Gregorian Decretals, it is really an independent collection, consisting, like the first authentic collection, of five *books* with their respective *titles* divided into *chapters*.

Hence the *mode of alleging* this collection is the same as that of the Gregorian compilation, with the sole difference that VI or 6° is substituted for X; hence: *c. i, 6°, I, 2* = chap. 1 (Liceat), in the Liber Sextus, book 1, title 2 de Constitutione.

2. The *juridical value* of the *Liber Sextus* is nearly the same as that of Gregory's Decretals, which were not abrogated by this collection. But it invalidated all the Decretals issued between Sept. 5, 1234, and Dec. 24, 1294, and not inserted in the "*Sextus*" or reserved, *i. e.,* indicated as such. The "*Regulae Juris*" have no legal value.[29]

ARTICLE 4

CLEMENTINAE (1317)

1. As the troublesome times required, Clement V published several constitutions, especially at the Council of Vienne in France (1313). He had them collected later, it seems, and sent to the two French universities of Orleans and Paris. This was after their promulgation at a public consistory held in the castle of Monteaux (de Montiliis), near Carpentras, in southern France. This collection, for some reason or other, was revoked by Clement himself, and only after his death (1314) were these Decretals, which had meanwhile been revised by "more skilful" hands, promulgated by his successor,

[29] Schulte, *l. c.,* II, p. 4; Friedberg, *C. J. C.,* II, 935 f.

John XXII, in the Bull "Quoniam nulla," October 25th, 1317. This collection is styled in the manuscripts "*Liber Septimus*," but owing to the influence of the glossators, the title was soon changed into "Constitutiones Clementinae" or simply "Clementinae." [30]

2. MATTER, ARRANGEMENT AND LEGAL VALUE.—With the exception of two decretals, one of Urban IV and one of Boniface VIII, all the "*Clementinae*" belong to the first Pope of the so-called "Babylonian Captivity." These decretals are, like the two preceding collections, divided into five *books*, and these into *titles* and *chapters*, the sum total of the latter being 106. The *mode of quoting the Clementinae* is, with the exception of the characteristic sign "*Clem.*," the same as that of the Gregorian or Bonifacian Decretals, *viz.: c. 1, Clem. I, 2 de rescriptis* = chapter 1, Clementinae, book 1, title 2 de rescriptis; or, as in the ancient canonists, cap. Abbates, Clem. (de rescriptis, which is not seldom omitted).

John XXII in his Bull of publication commands the addressees to receive these Decretals with good will (*prompto affectu*) and to make use of them in future "in the courts and schools" (*in judiciis et scholis*). Hence the *Clementinae* enjoy the same *authentic* valor as the decretals of Gregory IX and Boniface VIII. But it must be added that the other decretals which issued from the Apostolic See after the Bonifacian collection but not inserted or mentioned in the *Clementinae*, did not lose their legal value because the *Clementinae* contain

---

30 Cfr. Schulte, *Quellen*, II, 451 ff.; *Corpus Iuris Can.*, ed. Friedberg, II, Prol., pp. LVII ff. Joannes Andreae in his *glossa ad verbum* "*de caetero*" *in Const.* "*Quoniam nulla*" narrates that Clement V himself revoked the collection on account of some decretals being too long, others faulty, others unsuitable, and that these mistakes were then corrected by "more skilled hands"; that John XXII changed them cannot be proved.

no invalidating clause with regard to them, as was the case in the Bull of Boniface VIII, " Sacrosanctae." [31]

ARTICLE 5

EXTRAVAGANTES

1. Pope John XXII published several important constitutions, touching chiefly upon beneficiary subjects, not contained in the *Clementinae* and yet commented on by the glossators. Thus William de Monte Laudano had furnished "*glossae*" on three decretals of the aforesaid Pope: "*Sedes apostolica,*" "*Suscepti regiminis,*" and "*Execrabilis,*" issued in the first year of John's pontificate (1317). Zenzelinus de Cassanis also composed glosses on these three constitutions and, besides, on seventeen others of the same Pontiff, in the year 1325. These *twenty* decretals became known as the "*Decretales extravagantes, quae emanaverunt post Sextum,*" or later as "*Extravagantes Johannis XXII.*" They were divided into 14 *titles* and 20 *chapters.*[32]

2. These "*Extravagantes*" were published by JOHN CHAPPUIS in 1501 and 1503, together with some other decretals which had emanated from the Holy See, from John XXII to Sixtus IV. Out of these materials Chappuis made a collection, which he called "*Extravagantes Communes,*" in five *books* with *titles* and *chapters.* However, the fourth book (*De Matrimonio*) is missing, for lack of materials. The whole collection is poorly digested and cannot claim authenticity as a collection, though the decretals taken singly have the authority due to pontifical laws, as far as they are still in force (*v. g.,* "*Ambitiosae*" in III, 4).[33]

31 Laurin, *l. c.*, pp. 202 f.   33 Laurin, *l. c.*, p. 202.
32 Schulte, *op. cit.*, II, 59 f.

Mode of quoting:

　c. 2, Extr. Joannis XXII, tit. I (suscepti regiminis),
　c. un. Extr. Comm. III, 4 (Ambitiosae).

ARTICLE 6

THE "CORPUS JURIS CANONICI"

After having considered the several collections which were all published after the art of printing had been invented, either in five or in three volumes, a word must be added concerning the whole body of them, known as "*Corpus Juris Canonici.*"

I. "*Corpus Juris*" was a term applied at first to any body of laws, and later, in the twelfth century, to the collection of civil laws.[34]　In a Brief of Gregory XIII, "Quum pro munere pastorali," July 1, 1580, the collection containing the *Decretum Gratiani*, the *Decretales Gregorii*, the *Decretales Bonifacii*, the *Clementinae* and the two *Extravagantes* was styled "*Corpus Juris Canonici.*" Hence, in a *wider sense*, these five collections may be said to constitute the *Corpus.*

In the *strict sense*, however, the title can be applied only to the three *authentic* collections, *viz.:* to the Decretals of Gregory IX and Boniface VIII, and the *Clementinae.*　The nomenclature "*Corpus Juris Canonici Clausum*" is arbitrary and without foundation.[35]

2. If we regard the *structure* or make-up of the C. J. C. in its strict sense, *i. e.*, of the three authentic collections, we find inscriptions prefixed to the single titles as well

---

[34] Kipp, *Gesch. d. Quellen d. Röm. Rechts,* 1909, 168; v. Scherer, I, 270.

[35] Benedict XIV, " *Jam fere sex-* · *tus* " (*Bullarium,* ed. Mechlin, 1826, I, XIV); Laurin, *l. c.,* pp. 19, 25, 225 f.

as to the chapters, which latter, moreover, have summaries put immediately before the text.

a) Concerning the *inscriptions* above the *titles* there is a twofold class. Some exhibit simply the subject they treat of, *v. g., De Consuetudine* (I, 4), while others are longer and offer a clause or sentence complete in meaning, *v. g., "Ne sede vacante aliquid innovetur"* (X, III, 9). The former inscriptions have no legal value, whereas the latter have.

b) The *"summaria"* placed at the head of nearly every chapter are additions of the glossators and, therefore, destitute of legal value.

c) Neither legal nor historical merit can be attached to the *indications* of the *sources* whence the composer pretends to have borrowed his matter.

d) As to the *text* itself, juridical value can be attributed only to the *pars decisiva* or *dispositiva,* regardless of whether the source is genuine or spurious, but not to the narrative part or to the allegations of the contending parties.[36]

3. Mention must be made of the various *editions* of the *Corpus Juris Canonici* which are not all of equal authority.

a) *Authentic* is the edition published after the commission consisting of six cardinals and fifteen "doctors" had corrected the *C. J. C.* at the command of Gregory XIII in *Rome*, in 1582.[37] But the work of the "Correctores Romani," incomplete as it is, can claim only doctrinal value.[38] However, the Roman edition had the distinction that it could be quoted in the ecclesiastical courts as well as outside of them.[39]

---

[36] Wernz, *Jus Decretalium,* I, 325 f.
[37] Theiner, *l. c.,* app. I, pp. 3 f.
[38] Laurin, *l. c.,* p. 69.
[39] Greg. XIII., *"Quum pro munere,"* July 1, 1580; Friedberg, II, p. LXXXII.

b) Of purely *private authority* were the editions made
by the brothers PIERRE and FRANÇOIS PITHOU, at Paris
in 1687. The same holds good of the critical edition of
JUSTUS H. BÖHMER, Halle, 1747, whose " emendations "
are not always happy.[40]   For official purposes these editions are useless.

Better and worthy of attention is the edition which
EMIL FREDERICK RICHTER published at Leipsic in 1839.
He used the Roman edition as basis and added textual
corrections of his own.   This edition can be safely used
in practice, although it is not authentic.

A later critical edition is that of EMIL FRIEDBERG, published in two 4to volumes under the title, *Corpus Juris
Canonici.* Vol. I, 1879, contains the *Decretum Magistri
Gratiani,* Vol. II, 1881, the Decretals and Extravagantes.   This edition is based on extensive MS. researches, but neglects the Roman edition and omits all
glosses, though inserting the *partes decisae.*

40 Friedberg, II, XLII.

SECTION 3

SOURCES OF THE LAST PERIOD

1. After the golden age of Canon Law, resplendent with works and authors some of whom shall be mentioned later, there was a setting of the sun, until the *Council of Trent* seemed to breathe new life into the half-motionless frame of the Church at large and the skeleton of canonistic science in particular.

This gathering of learned men had, of course, for its chief aim not a reform of laws, but of morals. Still discipline and morals cannot easily be separated, and hence we see that the Council, especially in its third period, issued many important , enactments bearing directly on Canon Law. These *decrees* form a real *source* of Canon Law. Pius IV confirmed them and ordained that, after they had been duly promulgated in the city of Rome, legal force should be attributed to them from the first day of May, 1564.[1]

2. But, surprising though it be, it is a fact that, at least to our knowledge, there exists *no authentic collection of these decrees.* Some private editions were even placed on the Index.

The most noteworthy editions are:

a) AUG. BARBOSA's "*Collectanea Bullarii aliarumve Summ. PP. Constitutionum nec non Praecipuarum Decisionum, quae ab Apost. Sede et s. Congregationibus*

---

1 Constitutions of Pius IV: "*Sicut ad sacrorum*," July 18, 1564; "*Benedictus Deus*," Jan. 26, 1564. — The promulgation was made at the Lateran, St. Peter's, the Apost. Chancery, the Campo de' Fiori; exception was made for the "Tametsi" (c. 1, sess. 24 de ref. mat.).

S.R.E. usque ad a. 1633 emanaverunt," Lyons, 1634 (formerly on the Index).[2]

b) JOHN GALLEMART'S *"Concilium Tridentinum cum Declarationibus Cardinalium ejusdem Interpretum,"* ed. Guerra, Venetiis 1780, 2 Vols. (formerly on the Index).

c) RICHTER and SCHULTE'S *" Canones et Decreta Concilii Tridentini ex ed. Rom. a. 1834 repetiti,"* Berlin, 1864 (repr. Naples, 1869).[3]

3. Towards the close of the sixteenth century an attempt was made to gather the three authentic collections of Gregory IX, Boniface VIII, and Clement V into one body together with the decrees of the V Lateran and the Tridentine councils. Cardinal Pinello offered an undigested digest, which he styled *" Liber Septimus,"* to Clement VIII, in 1598, whence it was also called: *" Ssmi. D. N. Clementis P. VIII Decretales."* However, the Pope declined the offer and Pinello's work, though printed, was never promulgated.[4]

This was the last effort to codify the laws of the Church, until PIUS X, of happy memory (*" Arduum sane,"* March 19, 1904), instituted his commission, to which we owe the New Code.

4. After the Council of Trent (1563) the legislative activity of the Popes was by no means stayed. But this period, owing to a more intensified centralization, made it imperative for the Pontiff not to divide but rather to distribute his power among various tribunals and congregations which came into existence soon after the Council. Thus the channel of laws, as it were, was twofold: constitutions and decisions.

2 H. Reusch, *Der Index*, II, 74.

3 Concerning the history of the Council of Trent see Pallavicini, *Istoria del Concilio di Trento*, 1666; and *Concilium Tridentinum*, published by the Görresgesellschaft, Herder, 1901 ff.

4 Sentis, *Clem. VIII. Decretales*, 1870; v. Scherer, I, 275.

a) The *Constitutions* emanated chiefly in the form of Bulls, sometimes also in the form of Briefs, directly from the Pontiff and touched upon matters of importance for the Church at large. These have so far not been published in an authentic collection. All the so-called *Bullaria*, with the exception of that of Benedict XIV,[5] are of a purely private character. The chief *Bullaria* are:

α) L. CHERUBINI'S *Bullarium seu Collectio Diversarum Constitutionum Multorum Pontificum a Gregorio VII usque ad Sixtum V*, Rome, 1586. The second and third editions of this work comprised the constitutions of the Popes from Leo I to Paul V, to which ANGELUS A LANTUSCA and JOHN PAUL A ROMA added those from Urban VIII to Clement X (Rome, 1672).

AND. BARBERI and ALEX. SPETIA published the so-called *Continuatio Bullarii* (Clement XIII to Gregory XVI), Rome, 1825–57.[6] Here must also be mentioned the *Acta Pii IX*, 1854 ff. and the *Acta Leonis XIII*, 1881 ff., which, however, appear to lack authentic character, whilst the *Acta Pii X* (Vatican Press, 1907 ff.) are authentic and official.

β) *Bullarium Luxemburgense* (first printed at Geneva), or *Bullarium Magnum Romanum a Leone I ad Benedictum XIV*, 1717–28.

γ) *Turinense* (Al. Tomasetti), *Diplomatum et Privileg. S.R. Pont. a Leone I ad Clement. XII editio*, 1857–72, without critical discernment and with a great number of printing errors.

Mention must here be made of P. COUSTANT, *Epistolae RR. Pontificum a Clem. I ad Innoc. I*, Paris, 1721; AND. THIEL, *Epistolae RR. PP. Genuinae ab Hilario ad Pelagium II*, 1868. Of value are also the *Regesta* edited by

5 "*Jam fere sextus*," 1746, sent to Bologna University.

6 Coquelines, *Bullarum Amplissima Collectio*, Rome, 1739–44.

JAFFÉ, LÖWENFELD, PFLUGK-HARTUNG, EWALD-HART-
MANN (Greg. I.), and P. F. KEHR.

b) The *decrees* and *decisions* of the *Roman Congregations,* especially those of the Congr. of the Council, were
collected and published. The only *authentic collections,*
however, are the following:

S. Rit. C. Decreta Authentica, Rome, 1898–1912, 6
Vols.

Collectanea S. C. de Propaganda Fide, Rome, 1907, 2
Vols.

The collection of decrees of the Congr. of the Council,
which ran first under the name of " Libri Decretorum,"
from 1573 on were gathered in the *Thesaurus Resolu-
tionum S.C.C.* 1718 (resp. 1745) to 1908, in 167 vols.
Strictly private collections are ZAMBONI's *Coll. Declara-
tionum S.C.C.,* Atrebati, 1868, 4 Vols.; PALLOTINI, *Coll.
Omnium Concl. et Resolv.,* 1564–84 (alphabetic);
LINGEN and REUSS, *Causae Selectae,* Ratisbon, 1871.
There are also many scattered volumes of decisions of
the S. R. R.[7]

STUDY OF CANON LAW

It would be worth while to enter the studio of one of
those learned canonists of the past in order to observe
his way of studying, not only Canon Law, but also civil
law, from which was borrowed the method of applying
Canon Law (" *ordinem placitandi ex legibus* "). Then
we might enter a law school and learn their manner of
teaching. There, in the midst of hundreds of disciples,

[7] Besides the authors mentioned
above, the student may consult:
Doujat, *Praenotionum Canonicarum
libri quinque,* Venice, 1769; Sarti,
O. Camal., *De Claris Archigymnasii*
Bononiensis Professoribus, Rome,
1768, t. I; Savigny, *Geschichte des
Röm. Rechts im Mittelalter,* 1834–
54, Vols. III and IV.

eagerly intent on the teacher's words, a *Decretum* might be seen on the professor's table. First, with a sonorous voice, he reads the *summary* of the chapter he is about to expound. After that follows the *reading* of the *litera, i. e.,* the text of the chapter (or canon), with distinct accentuation and more slowly, that the students might be enabled to take down the wording in case they could not, because of poverty (books at that time were rare and expensive), or for other reasons, acquire the volume. Then the *litera,* if necessary,[8] is corrected, which was called *emendatio literae.* Hereupon the proper work of the teacher began — the *exposition* or expounding of the canon. This work comprised different acts: *Contradictions* were pointed out and solved by the method assigned by the " magister," then followed *casuistry* and corroboration of the explanation given and other *arguments* taken from the Decree or other sources.

The *students* under the supervision of the teacher are busy at work, engaged partly in *repetitions,* partly in *disputations.* The former are much like our modern " seminars," in which postgraduates or aspirants to the laurea expound some particular text more elaborately. *Disputations* were held *diebus Mercurii* (Wednesdays), and conducted in scholastic style — sometimes, we fear, to extravagance.

This method of training, if kept up from six to ten years, was apt to produce *thorough scholars* and future " masters," which title towards the end of the twelfth century was changed to " *doctors.*" Note must be taken of the fact that the universities, being few in number, attracted the cream of professors and were efficient in maintaining a choice staff. The *clerical* character of

8 Cfr. Huguccio's *Glossa* on c. 31, C. 2, q. 6.

these flourishing schools, endowed by Popes and Bishops with benefices and other sources of revenue, was carefully maintained and proved no hindrance to effective teaching, intense study, and good morals.[9]

[9] Cfr. Schulte, *Quellen*, I, pp. 111 ff.; 196; II, pp. 214 f., 493, etc.

SECTION 4

THE GLOSSATORS

If we call the epoch extending from the appearance of Gratian's *Decretum* to the Council of Trent the period of the Glossators, we look to the majority of writers (*denominatio fit a potiori*) without intending to exclude other writers and writings of a different kind.

1. Mention was made of the method the teachers were wont to employ in school. It was but natural that the work of the school should not be confined within the school-walls but also prove a fertile soil for literary products. These are, to a great extent at least, still preserved, either in the form of *Glossae,* or in the more stately shape of *Summae* and *Tractatus.*

In order of time the *Glossae* were the first literary output of the followers of the Master. A gloss [1] or verbal explanation was generally placed above the word to be explained, and therefor, called *glossa interlinearis.* Not rarely these glosses were placed on the margin or at the bottom of the page (*glossae marginales*). If continuously applied to the whole text of the Decree or the Decretals, such a series was styled *apparatus.*

Some authors, *v. g.* Bernardus Papiensis, preferred another way, *viz.:* that of writing commentaries, called *Summae.* These either followed the order of the text

[1] From the Greek γλῶσσα (lingua); "*dicitur expositio sententiae literam continuans et exponens, unde dicitur glossa, i. e., lingua.*" Doujat, *l. c.,* l, V, c. 2, n. 2.

52

(Decree or Decretals) closely and uninterruptedly, or left the order of the text and exhibited only a summary, using the text for the sake of proof. In this latter case they might just as well be called *Tractatus*, although these, properly speaking, were rather essays on some particular subject (*v. g.* Durantis' " Ordo Judiciarius "). It is sometimes difficult to distinguish between *Summae* and *Tractatus.*[2] The glossators had the custom of distinguishing their glosses from those of others by certain initials or *sigla, v. g.* Huguccio used H., Bartholomaeus of Brescia, B. or Bart., etc.

2. We will name some of the most noteworthy glossators and authors of canonical works, retaining their Latin names, as they were then known. To the *Decretum* JOANNES FAVENTINUS composed an apparatus about 1179–87. CARDINALIS introduced the *jus civile* into the Decree. BAZIANUS (+ 1197) in his glosses employed the decretals. The famous " *Glossa Ordinaria* " was furnished by JOHANNES TEUTONICUS, about the year 1215. A rich glossary based upon the preceding and on the compilations is that of BARTHOLOMAEUS BRIXIENSIS, about 1240–45; it is the last gloss on the *Decretum*.[3]

The *Decretales Gregorii* were glossed by VINCENTIUS HISPANUS and BERNARDUS PARMENSIS DE BOTONE (+ 1263), whose *glossa* is called " *ordinaria.*"

The " *Liber Sextus* " and the " *Clementinae* " were adorned with the glosses of JOANNES ANDREAE (+ 1348), one of the most illustrious canonists, " *fons et tuba juris,*" as he was called.[4]

3. SUMMAE AND TRACTATUS.—An entire catalogue would be necessary to do justice to the galaxy of writers who flourished from the twelfth to the fifteenth

2 Schulte, *Quellen,* I, 219.
3 *Ib.,* I, 145, 191, 172; II, 86 f.
4 His daughter Novella also taught Canon Law,— but behind a curtain!

century. We select the best known without wishing to detract from the fame of the others. *Summa Magistri Rolandi* (Bandinelli), later Pope Alexander III; [5] *Summa Rufini*, about 1166; *Summa Stephani Tornacensis* (1203); *Summa Simonis de Bisiano*, made about 1174–79; *Summa Huguccionis*, about 1187; *Summa Bernardi Papiensis*, about 1191–98; this is a sort of compendium of Canon Law.[6]

What were called *Lecturae* were in fact commentaries, and might also be styled *Summae*. Such were composed by *Innocent IV* (Sinibaldus Fliscus, 1243–54), "*Apparatus in quinque libros Decretalium*"; HOSTIENSIS (Henricus de Seguesia, + 1271), "*Lectura in Gregorii IX Decretales*"; ABBAS ANTIQUUS, "*Lectura seu Apparatus ad Decretales Gregorii IX*," composed about 1270; ÆGIDIUS DE FUSCARARIIS (1289); JOANNES GARSIAS HISPANUS (c. 1282); GUIDO DE BAYSIO, "*Commentarius in Sextum*" (c. 1299–1312); GUILIELMUS DE MONTE LAUDANO (1343), "*Lecturae super Sextum, Clementinas et tres Extravagantes Joannis XXII*"; ZENZELINUS DE CASSANIS (the same). Of great authority are the following: PETRUS DE ANCHARANO (1416), FRANCISCUS DE ZABARELLIS (1417), ANTONIUS DE BUTRIO (1408), JOANNES AB IMOLA (1436), and especially PANORMITANUS, also called Nicolaus de Tudeschis, O.S.B., Abbas Modernus or Abbas Siculus (+ 1453),— all of whom composed commentaries on the Decretals and the *Clementinae*.

The following works rather resemble treatises or essays:

BERNARDUS PAPIENSIS, "*Summa de Matrimonio;*" "*Summa de Electione;*" TANCRED, "*Summa de Sponsalibus et Matrimonio*," and "*Ordo Judiciarius;*" WIL-

LIAM OF DURANT (1296), called "SPECULATOR," "*Speculum Legatorum*," "*Speculum Judiciale*," "*Rationale Divinorum Officiorum.*"[7]

Some works are especially concerned with the *papal power*, which was, at times, rather insipidly defended. To this class belong: JOANNES PARISIENSIS (+ 1306), "*Tractatus de Regia Potestate et Papali*"; ÆGIDIUS ROMANUS (Colonna, + 1315), "*De Excellentia Pontificatus*," "*De Potestate Ecclesiastica libri tres*," "*De Regimine Principum*"; AUGUSTINUS TRIUMPHUS (+ 1328), "*Summa de Potestate Ecclesiastica*";[8] RODERIC SANCIUS DE AREVALO (+ 1470), "*Defensorium Status Ecclesiastici*," "*De Monarchia Orbis*" (the Pope is the monarch of the whole universe); JOHN A TURRECREMATA (+ 1468), "*De Potestate Papae et Concilii Generalis Auctoritate;*" THOMAS DE VIO (CAJETAN) (+ 1534), "*De Auctoritate et Potestate Rom. Pont.*," "*De Auctoritate Conciliorum.*" Of some interest are the works of DOMINICUS DE DOMINICIS (+ 1478), "*De Reformationibus Romanae Curiae*," "*De Cardinalium Electione et Legitima Creatione*," etc.[9]

[7] Edited, respectively, by Wunderlich, 1841, and Bergmann, 1842.

[8] Cfr. Scholz, *Publisistik sur Zeit Philipps des Schönen*, K.-R. Abhandl. v. Stutz, 1903, 618.

[9] Cfr. Schulte, *Quellen*, II, passim.

SECTION 5

The reformation initiated by the Council of Trent was vigorously carried out by the later Popes, who proved themselves excellent legislators. The tendency of gravitation towards the centre became more accentuated. This is very noticeable in Canon Law. Besides this *centralizing* tendency there are two other characteristics which single out this period from those preceding. Humanism invaded the realm of law on a side where it was particularly vulnerable by introducing *historical criticism*. This operation was no detriment to the science, but it might have proved dangerous in the hands of an unskilful surgeon. It has produced works of great and lasting merit.

Another innovation, less necessary and rather cumbersome, is the *moralizing* strain now brought into Canon Law. This was a disadvantage because it obscured the character of the Church as a public society and made the law appear to be an appendix of the confessional. The moralists entered into the vineyard of Canon Law and — but *melius est silere quam loqui.*

The following list may serve students especially in their selection of canonical books. The works may be divided into historico-critical writings, commentaries, and manuals; those which, for one reason or another, are preferred at the Roman Curia are marked with an asterisk.

56

1. HISTORICO-CRITICAL WRITINGS

Besides the authors mentioned above the following may be recommended:

CARD. JOHN BAPTIST PITRA, O.S.B., "*Juris Ecclesiastici Graecorum Historia et Monumenta,*" Rome, 1864-68; "*Analecta Novissima Spicilegii Solesmensis,*" Tusculi, 1885; L. THOMASSIN, "*Vetus et Nova Eccles. Disciplina circa Beneficia,*" Magontiaci, 1787; E. LOENING, *Geschichte des deutschen Kirchenrechts,* 1878, 2 vols. (still a standard work).

2. COMMENTARIES

Although not a commentary in the proper sense, yet as embracing almost the whole range of Canon Law, we must mention the works of the "*Princeps Canonistarum,*"[1] BENEDICT XIV, whose *Opera Omnia* (Prati, 1839 ff.) are a rich source of information.

A. BARBOSA, *Opera Omnia,* Lugdun., 1660.

C. S. BERARDI, "*Commentaria in Jus Eccl. Universum,*" Taurini, 1766 (critical).

DE ANGELIS, "*Praelectiones Juris Canonici,*" Rome, 1877 ff.

L. FERRARIS, "*Prompta Bibliotheca Canonica,*" etc., various editions, the latest by J. Bucceroni, S.J., Romae, 1885-99, 9 Vols., but with little improvement as to dates of the decisions of the S. Congregations.

*CARD. VINCENT PETRA (+ 1747), "*Commentaria in Constitutiones Apostolicas,*" Romae, 1705-1726, 5 Vols., besides "*De S. Poenitentiaria Apostolica,*" 1712.

E. PIRHING, S.J., "*Universum Jus Canonicum,*" Dillingae, 1674.

---

[1] Cfr. Hurter, *Nomenclator,* 3rd ed., Innsbruck, 1910, Vol. IV, col. 1595 sqq.

PICHLER, S.J., *"Jus Can. Universum,"* Ingolstadii, 1735.

*ANACLETUS REIFFENSTUEL, O.F.Min., *"Jus Canonicum Universum,"* Antwerpiae, 1743, 3 Vols.

*JOHN BAPT. RIGANTI, *"Commentaria in Regulas, Constitutiones et Ordinationes Cancellariae Apostolicae,"* Romae, 1744 (an important work for the Rules of the Apostolic Chancery).

SANTI-LEITNER, *"Praelectiones Juris Canonici,"* Ratisbonae, 1898 f.

*F. SCHMALZGRUEBER, S.J., *"Jus 'Eccl. Universum,"* Romae, 1843 ff., 12 Vols.

*GONZALEZ TELLEZ, *"Commentaria perpetua in singulos textus quinque lib. decretal. Gregorii IX,"* Lugduni, 1673.

WERNZ, S.J., *"Jus Decretalium,"* Romae, 1898 ff.

JOHN BAPT. CARD. DE LUCA (+ 1683), *"Theatrum Veritatis et Justitiae"* (a prolix work of motley content), Romae, 1671 f., 18 Vols.

3. MANUALS

AICHNER, *"Compendium Juris Eccl.,"* Innsbruck, 1895.

J. DEVOTI, *"Juris Canonici Universi Publ. et Privati libri quinque,"* Romae, 1803, 3 Vols. (still useful).

F. HEINER (S.R.R. Auditor), *"Katholisches Kirchenrecht,"* Paderborn, 1897.

JOS. LAURENTIUS, S.J., *"Institutiones Juris Ecclesiastici,"* Freiburg, 1903.

G. PHILLIPS, *"Kirchenrecht,"* 1845 ff., 8 Vols.

VON SCHERER, *"Handbuch d. Kirchenrechts,"* Graz, 1886, 2 Vols. (incomplete, but very thorough and critical).

J. F. Schulte, "*Lehrbuch d. Kath. Kirchenrechts,*" 1863.

S. B. Smith, "*Elements of Ecclesiastical Law,*" 1891, 3 Vols. These we have frequently consulted.

It may be permitted to add a few *Benedictine* authors.

Placidus Boekiin (+ 1752), "*Commentarius in Jus Canonicum Universum,*" 1735 f. (commentary-like and extensive).

*Lud. Engel (+ 1674 at Melk in Austria), "*Collegium Universi Juris Canonici,*" Salisburgi, 1671–74; Id., "*Tractatus de Privilegiis et Juribus Monasteriorum,*" *ibid.*

Martin Gerbert (S. Blasii, + 1793), "*Principia Theoriae Canonicae,*" 1758; "*De Communione Potestatis Ecclesiasticae inter Summos Ecclesiae Principes et Episcopos,*" 1761; "*De Legitima Ecclesiastica Potestate circa Sacra et Profana,*" 1761.

Rob. König (+ 1713), "*Principia Juris Can.,*" Salisburgi, 1691–97.

Maurus Schenkl (+ 1816), "*Institutiones Juris Eccl. Germaniae Accommodatae,*" Ingolstadii, 1760; Ratisbonae, 1853.

*Francis Schmier (+ 1728), "*Jurisprudentia Canonico-Civilis,*" Salisburgi, 1716.

Coel. Sfondrati (+ 1696), "*Regale Sacerdotium R. Pontifici Assertum,*" 1684; "*Gallia Vindicata,*" S. Galli, 1687.

Greg. Zallwein (+ 1766), "*Principia Juris Ecclesiastici Universalis et Particul. Germaniae,*" 1763 ·(considered one of the best manuals in its day).

CHAPTER V

Our gloriously reigning Holy Father Benedict XV, in his Bull of promulgation, refers to the Motu proprio "Arduum sane," which was issued by Pius X, March 17, 1904, and gave rise to the present Code. In that memorable pronouncement the late Pontiff stated the reasons which prompted him as the supreme Pastor of souls, who has the care of all the churches, to provide for a new codification of ecclesiastic laws, with a view "to put together with order and clearness all the laws of the Church thus far issued, removing all those that would be recognized as abrogated or obsolete, adapting others to the necessities of the times, and enacting new ones in conformity with the present needs." We leave it to the reader and the watchmen of Sion to judge whether this purpose has been achieved. A fair-minded and unbiassed critic will certainly acknowledge the juridical genius of H. E. Cardinal Gasparri, who bore the heaviest part of the burden, and of his zealous collaborators in getting up, within the short space of twelve years, a collection covering centuries of legislation and volumes of laws and commentaries. Those who will have to make practical use of the New Code will not fail to admire, first and above all, its brevity as well as the convenient arrangement of the matter and the clearness of the style. The canonist is grateful and in his heart will muse over Virgil's verse, "*Redeunt Saturnia regna,*" because, after a long period of relative neglect, his office again becomes important and, we dare say, necessary. For although the advantages of the New Code are undeniable, a commentary is necessary in order to grasp the full meaning of the text. This is evident from the fact that the Code embodies " *nova et vetera.*"

The old laws must be explained, according to the general rules of interpretation indeed, but also in harmony with the traditional significance that can be gathered only from an acquaintance with bygone ages and authors. This is plainly stated in canon 6, which reads:

" The 'Code for the most part retains the discipline thus far in use, although it also offers opportune changes. Hence: 1.° All laws, both universal or particular, which are opposed to the laws prescribed in this Code, are abrogated, with the exception of those particular laws for which express provision is made."

The term *law* is to be taken in the strict sense of a written enactment. Privileges are not included, for they are special, not particular, laws. The provision concerning particular laws must be expressly mentioned, at least in a general way. Cfr. Can. 1253 concerning feast-days, which is specially applicable to our country.

" 2.° Canons which state the old law unchanged, must be understood according to the authority of the old law and therefore according to the interpretations given by recognized authors.

" 3.° Canons which conform to the old law only in part, must be understood according to the old law as far as they agree with it; in so far as they differ from it, they must be explained in their own light.

" 4.° When there is doubt whether an enactment of the Code differs from the old law, the latter must be upheld."

These rules not only establish the continuity of the law, but also offer a key to the interpreter. It is evident that a society which has lasted for centuries cannot entirely overthrow and set aside all of its old laws.

Hence we find throughout the Code not only allusions to, but almost verbal restatements of, the old law. When the Code says " *ex integro*," which we translate by " unchanged," this term must be taken in its substantial, not verbal meaning. Thus, concerning postulation, the Code (Can. 180, § 2) is almost a repetition of the text of the *Corpus Juris*, though not *ad verbum*.

When a canon is divisible, *i. e.*, when it partly rehearses an old law, and partly gives new regulations, the interpretation and application must necessarily conform to the old law, as well as to the *ratio legis* and the wording of the newly enacted part, as shall appear more fully in the course of this Commentary. It were useless to set forth examples which occur in nearly every canon. But these rules show and clearly prove that even the new Code does not make the authority of the school superfluous or useless.

" 5.° All penalties not mentioned in this Code, of whatever denomination, spiritual, temporal, medicinal or vindictive (so called), whether *ferendae* or *latae sententiae*, are hereby abrogated."

The " Apostolicae Sedis " of Pius IX (1868) had a similar purpose, *i. e.*, to reduce the penal Code to a unit and to certain limits. The new Code embodies another attempt to simplify the penal law.

" 6.° As regards the other disciplinary laws thus far in use, those that are neither explicitly nor implicitly contained in this Code must be held to have lost obligatory force, unless they are found in approved liturgical books or are part of the divine law, either positive or natural."

This is another guiding line along which the interpreter has to move. With the exception of natural and divine positive law and such rules as are contained in the approved liturgical books (the Pontifical, the Missal, the Roman Ritual, and the *Ceremoniale Episcoporum*) all disciplinary laws made by human authority cease to be binding. The commentator may take illustrations from them, but is not allowed to confound them with the existing law or to represent them as still binding.

Having before our mind these wise rules, we shall, with God's help, endeavor to comply with them scrupulously and to follow the injunction of the S. C. Sem. et Stud., Aug. 7, 1917, concerning the teaching of Canon Law.[1]

It remains to point out the *division* of the new Code. It consists of five books, doubtless as a remembrance of the Decretals. However, a mere glance at the Code will convince the student that the real principle of division is the threefold time-honored one according to *personae, res,* and *actiones.* The first book contains all that was embraced in the first book of the Decretals and is here called " general rules," whilst the fourth and fifth books form one subject, *viz.:* the *actiones,* with this sole difference that procedure is separated from the penal code. The second book is entitled *De Personis,* and the third, *De Rebus.* But the ancient trilogy certainly is apparent in the new Code.

---

[1] *Acta Ap. Sedis,* IX, p. 439.

CONSTITUTION "PROVIDENTISSIMA" OF BENEDICT XV, PROMULGATING THE NEW CODE

To Our Venerable Brethren and Beloved Sons the Patriarchs, Primates, Archbishops, Bishops, and Other Ordinaries, and also to the Professors and Students of the Catholic Universities and Seminaries

BENEDICT, BISHOP

SERVANT OF THE SERVANTS OF GOD

FOR A PERPETUAL REMEMBRANCE OF THE MATTER

The most provident of mothers, the Church, enriched by her Divine Founder with all the notes befitting a perfect society, from the very beginning of her existence, when, obeying the mandate of the Lord, she commenced to teach and govern all nations, undertook to regulate and safeguard the discipline of the clergy and the Christian people by definite laws.

In process of time, however, particularly when she achieved her freedom and grew greater and more widespread from day to day, she never ceased to develop and unfold the right of making laws, which belongs to her by her very constitution. She did this by promulgating numerous and various decrees emanating from the Roman Pontiffs and Ecumenical Councils, as events and times suggested. By means of these laws and precepts she made wise provision for the government of the clergy and Christian people, and, as history bears witness, wonderfully promoted the welfare of the State and civilization.   For the Church was at pains not only to abrogate the laws of barbarous nations and to reduce their rude customs to civilized form, but, trusting in the assistance of the divine light, she tempered the Roman law itself, that wonderful monument of ancient wisdom, which has deservedly been called " written reason," and, having corrected its defects, perfected it in a Christian manner to such a degree that, as the ways of public and private life tended to greater perfection, abundant materials were supplied for the making of new laws both in the Middle Ages and more recent times.

However, owing to changes in the circumstances of the times and the necessities of men, as Our Predecessor of happy memory, Pius X, wisely declared in his Motu proprio " *Arduum sane,*" of March 17, 1904, Canon Law, no longer achieved its end with sufficient speed.   For in the passing of centuries a great many laws were issued, of which some were abrogated by the supreme authority of the Church or fell into desuetude, while others proved too difficult to enforce, as times changed, or ceased to be useful to the common good.   To these objections must be added that the laws of the Church had so increased in number and were so separated and scattered, that many of them were unknown, not only to the people, but to the most learned scholars as well.

Moved by these reasons, Our Predecessor of happy memory, at the very beginning of his Pontificate, considering how useful it would be for the restoration and strengthening of ecclesiastical discipline, if the serious inconveniences enumerated above were removed, decided to gather together and to digest with order and clearness all the laws of the Church issued down to our own day, removing all that were abrogated or obsolete, adapting others as far as needful to the necessities and customs of the present time,[1] and making new ones according as the need and opportunity should direct. When, after mature deliberation, he put his hand to this most difficult enterprise, he deemed it necessary to consult with the Bishops, whom the Holy Ghost has chosen to rule the Church of God, and to ascertain fully their views on the matter. Accordingly, he directed that, by letter from the Cardinal Secretary of State, all the Archbishops of the Catholic world should be invited to consult with their suffragan Bishops and other Ordinaries obliged to take part in Provincial Councils, and, after such consultation, to report to this Holy See what parts of the existing ecclesiastical law in their opinion stood in need of change or correction.[2]

Then, after having called upon numerous experts in Canon Law residing in Rome and other places to collaborate in the undertaking, he commanded Our Beloved Son, Cardinal Gasparri, then Archbishop of Caesarea, to direct, perfect, and, as far as necessary, complete the work of the consultors. He also instituted a Commission of Cardinals, naming as its members Cardinals Dominic Ferrata, Casimir Gennari, Benjamin Cavicchioni, Joseph Calasanctius Vives y Tuto, and Felix Cavagnis, who, in accordance with the suggestions of Our Beloved Son Cardinal Gasparri, should diligently examine the proposed canons, and change, correct, and perfect them as their judgment directed.[3] When these five men passed away, one after the other, there were appointed in their places Our Beloved Sons Cardinals Vincent Vannutelli,

---

1 Cfr. the Motu proprio "*Arduum sane*."

2 Cfr. the Epistle "*Pergratum mihi*," of March 25, 1904.

3 Cfr. the Motu proprio "*Arduum sane*."

Cajetan De Lai, Sebastian Martinelli, Basil Pompili, Cajetan Bisleti, William Van Rossum, Philip Giustini, and Michael Lega, who have admirably completed the work confided to them.

Finally, after again consulting the prudence and authority of all his Venerable Brethren in the Episcopate, he directed that to them and to all the Superiors of the Regular Orders, who are accustomed to be summoned to an Ecumenical Council, should be sent copies of the new Code finished and corrected, before promulgation, in order that they might freely manifest their observations on the proposed canons.[4]

But since, meanwhile, to the sorrow of the whole Catholic world, Our Predecessor of immortal memory passed out of this life, it became Our duty, as soon as by the secret will of Providence we began Our Pontificate, to receive with due honor the views thus collected from every quarter of those who with Us form the teaching Church. Then finally we acknowledged in all its parts, approved, and ratified the new Code of the whole of Canon Law, which had been petitioned for by many Bishops at the Vatican Council, and begun more than twelve years ago.

Therefore, having invoked the aid of Divine grace, and relying upon the authority of the Blessed Apostles Peter and Paul, of Our own accord and with certain knowledge, and in the fullness of the Apostolic power with which we are invested, by this Our Constitution, which we wish to be valid for all time, We promulgate, decree, and order that the present Code, just as it is compiled, shall have from this time forth the power of law for the Universal Church, and We confide it to your custody and vigilance.

4 Cfr. the Epistle " *De Mandato,*" of March 20, 1912.

But in order that all concerned may be able to have a thorough knowledge of the regulations of the Code before they begin to be binding, We ordain that they shall not come into effect until Pentecost day next year, *i. e.,* May 19th, 1918.

Notwithstanding all contrary regulations, constitutions, privileges, even those worthy of special and individual mention, and notwithstanding contrary customs, even though they be immemorial, or whatever else may run counter to this Constitution.

For no one, therefore, is it lawful willingly to contradict or rashly to disobey in any way this Our constitution, ordination, limitation, suppression or derogation. If any one should dare to do so, let him know that he will incur the wrath of Almighty God and of the Blessed Apostles Peter and Paul.

Given at Rome, from St. Peter's, on the Feast of Pentecost of the year one thousand nine hundred and seventeen, the third year of Our Pontificate.

PETER CARD. GASPARRI,
    Secretary of State

               O. CARD. CAGIANO DE AZEVEDO,
               Chancellor of the H. R. Church.

PROFESSION OF FAITH PRESCRIBED BY THE NEW CODE

Ego *N.* firma fide credo et profiteor omnia et singula, quae continentur in symbolo Fidei, quo sancta Romana Ecclesia utitur, videlicet: Credo in unum Deum, Patrem omnipotentem, factorem caeli et terrae, visibilium omnium et invisibilium. Et in unum Dominum Iesum Christum, Filium Dei Unigenitum. Et ex Patre natum, ante omnia saecula.— Deum de Deo, lumen de lumine, Deum verum de Deo vero. Genitum non factum, consubstantialem Patri: per quem omnia facta sunt. Qui propter nos homines, et propter nostram salutem descendit de caelis. Et incarnatus est de Spiritu Sancto ex Maria Virgine, et Homo factus est. Crucifixus etiam pro nobis, sub Pontio Pilato: passus, et sepultus est. Et resurrexit tertia die, secundum Scripturas. Et ascendit in caelum: sedet ad dexteram Patris. Et iterum venturus est cum gloria iudicare vivos, et mortuos: cuius regni non erit finis. Et in Spiritum Sanctum, Dominum et vivificantem: qui ex Patre Filioque procedit. Qui cum Patre et Filio simul adoratur, et conglorificatur: qui locutus est per prophetas. Et Unam, Sanctam, Catholicam et Apostolicam Ecclesiam. Confiteor unum Baptisma in remissionem peccatorum. Et exspecto resurrectionem mortuorum. Et vitam venturi saeculi. Amen.

Apostolicas et ecclesiasticas traditiones, reliquasque eiusdem Ecclesiae observationes et constitutiones firmissime admitto et amplector. Item sacram Scripturam iuxta eum sensum, quem tenuit et tenet sancta Mater

Ecclesia, cuius est iudicare de vero sensu et interpretatione sacrarum Scripturarum, admitto; nec eam unquam, nisi iuxta unanimem consensum Patrum, accipiam et interpretabor.

Profiteor quoque septem esse vere et proprie Sacramenta novae legis a Iesu Christo Domino nostro instituta, atque ad salutem humani generis, licet non omnia singulis, necessaria, scilicet, Baptismum, Confirmationem, Eucharistiam, Poenitentiam, Extremam Unctionem, Ordinem et Matrimonium; illaque gratiam conferre, et ex his Baptismum, Confirmationem et Ordinem sine sacrilegio reiterari non posse.— Receptos quoque et approbatos Ecclesiae Catholicae ritus in supradictorum omnium Sacramentorum sollemni administratione recipio et admitto.— Omnia et singula quae de peccato originali et de iustificatione in sacrosancta Tridentina Synodo definita et declarata fuerunt, amplector et recipio.— Profiteor pariter in Missa offerri Deo verum, proprium et propitiatorium Sacrificium pro vivis et defunctis; atque in sanctissimo Eucharistiae Sacramento esse vere, realiter et substantialiter Corpus et Sanguinem una cum anima et divinitate Domini nostri Iesu Christi, fierique conversionem totius substantiae panis in Corpus, et totius substantiae vini in Sanguinem, quam conversionem Catholica Ecclesia Transsubstantiationem appellat. Fateor etiam sub altera tantum specie totum atque integrum Christum, verumque Sacramentum sumi.— Constanter teneo Purgatorium esse, animasque ibi detentas fidelium suffragiis iuvari. Similiter et Sanctos una cum Christo regnantes venerandos atque invocandos esse, eosque orationes Deo pro nobis offerre, atque eorum Reliquias esse venerandas. Firmiter assero imagines Christi ac Deiparae semper Virginis, necnon aliorum Sanctorum habendas et retinendas

esse, atque eis debitum honorem ac venerationem imper-
tiendam.— Indulgentiarum etiam potestatem a Christo in
Ecclesia relictam fuisse, illarumque usum Christiano
populo maxime salutarem esse affirmo.— Sanctam, Catholicam et Apostolicam Romanam Ecclesiam, omnium Ec-
clesiarum matrem et magistram agnosco, Romanoque
Pontifici beati Petri Apostolorum Principis successori ac
Iesu Christi Vicario veram obedientiam spondeo ac iuro.

Cetera item omnia a sacris Canonibus et Oecumenicis
Conciliis, ac praecipue a sacrosancta Tridentina Synodo
et ab Oecumenico Concilio Vaticano tradita, definita ac
declarata, praesertim de Romani Pontificis primatu et
infallibili magisterio, indubitanter recipio atque profiteor,
simulque contraria omnia, atque haereses quascunque ab
Ecclesia damnatas et reiectas et anathematizatas, ego pariter damno, reiicio et anathematizo. Hanc veram Catholicam Fidem, extra quam nemo salvus esse potest, quam
in praesenti sponte profiteor et veraciter teneo, eandem
integram et inviolatam usque ad extremum vitae spiritum,
constantIssIme, Deo adiuvante, retinere et confiteri, atque
a meis subditis seu illis, quorum cura ad me in munere
meo spectabit, teneri et doceri et praedicari, quantum in
me erit curaturum, ego idem N. spondeo, voveo ac iuro.
Sic me Deus adiuvet, et haec sancta Dei Evangelia.

PART II
COMMENTARY

BOOK I

GENERAL RULES

CAN. 1

Licet in Codice iuris canonici Ecclesiae quoque Orientalis disciplina saepe referatur, ipse tamen unam respicit Latinam Ecclesiam, neque Orientalem obligat, nisi de iis agatur, quae ex ipsa rei natura etiam Orientalem afficiunt.

Though the discipline of the Oriental Church is often referred to in the Code of Canon Law, the Code itself regards only the Latin Church and does not bind the Oriental Church except in matters which of their very nature concern also the latter.

In other words, the new Code binds the Oriental Church only in so far as its dicipline is expressly mentioned therein.

This point was decided in 1907 by the Sacred Congregation of the Propaganda in a decree which touches upon the binding force of the Constitutions of the Holy See.[1]

1 Cf. *Collectanea P. F.*, 1907, II, n. 1578.

This decree establishes that laws emanating from the Holy See are binding upon the Oriental Church,

a) if they concern matters of faith or morals;

b) if they contain matters connected with the divine or the natural law, *e. g.*, the application of Holy Mass for the people at least sometimes during the year;

c) if the laws themselves expressly state that they are meant to bind the Oriental Church.

The Oriental Churches are distinguished from the Latin Church by their respective liturgical rites,[2] whilst in faith or dogma they are united with the Roman Pontiff. To the Oriental Church belong eight large groups with their respective subdivisions: the Byzantine Uniats with the Melchites, the Ruthenians, the Bulgarians, the Rumanians, the Italo-Greeks (in Calabria and Sicily), the Chaldees, the Copts, the Abyssinians, the Catholic Syrians, the Maronites, and the Armenians and Uniats of Malabar. The Oriental Catholics living in the U. S. remain subject to their respective Church, so far as rite is concerned, but in disciplinary matters, *v. g.*, celibacy of the clergy, they follow the Latin Church.

CAN. 2

Codex, plerumque, nihil decernit de ritibus et caeremoniis quas liturgici libri, ab Ecclesia Latina probati, servandas praecipiunt in celebratione sacrosancti Missae sacrificii, in administratione Sacramentorum et Sacramentalium aliisque sacris peragendis. Quare omnes liturgicae leges vim suam retinent, nisi earum aliqua in Codice expresse corrigantur.

2 Cf. *Cath. Encyclopedia*, Vol. V, *s. v.* Eastern Churches. The Orientals also gain indulgences like the Latins (S. Poenit., 7 July, 1917, *A. Ap. S.*, 1917, ix, p. 399).

The Code, furthermore, decrees nothing about the rites and ceremonies which the liturgical books approved by the Latin Church prescribe for the celebration of the most holy Sacrifice of the Mass, the administration of the Sacraments and sacramentals, and other sacred functions. Hence all liturgical laws retain their force unless expressly corrected in the Code.

See Introduction, *supra,* pp. 60 sqq.

Can. 3

Codicis canones initas ab Apostolica Sede cum variis Nationibus conventiones nullatenus abrogant aut iis aliquid abrogant; eae idcirco perinde ac in praesens vigere pergent, contrariis huius Codicis praescriptis minime obstantibus.

The canons of the Code in no wise abrogate or derogate from the agreements entered into between the Apostolic See and different nations; these agreements therefore remain in full force, notwithstanding contrary prescriptions of the Code.

This canon is evidently intended for those countries which maintain a so-called diplomatic or juridical relation with the Holy See. Where there is complete separation between Church and State, this canon does not apply, and hence the United States and England are not directly affected. We say *directly;* for, if one of the countries in which the aforesaid separation prevails should acquire a territory, or part thereof, which had a concordat with the Holy See, it would be obliged to abide by the concordat until the case could be legally settled with the Apostolic See (Congregation of Extraordinary Affairs).[3] An instance of a peaceful settlement is that with the United States concerning the Philippine Islands.

CAN. 4

Iura aliis quaesita, itemque privilegia atque indulta quae, ab Apostolica Sede ad haec usque tempora personis sive physicis sive moralibus concessa, in usu adhuc sunt nec revocata, integra manent, nisi huius Codicis canonibus expresse revocentur.

Rights otherwise acquired, as well as privileges and indults hitherto granted by the Apostolic See either to individuals or to organizations remain intact if they are still in use and have not been revoked, unless expressly revoked in the canons of this Code.

The rights here mentioned are the so-called *jura quaesita*,[4] *i. e.*, the legally acquired subjective rights of a third person. For instance, a bishop has the right of appointing one to a certain office; hence, though a corporation (monastery) has the right of appointing one of its members, this appointee must be presented to the Ordinary. *Indults* are faculties granted by the Holy See, *e. g.*,

---

3 A concordat (*conventio*) is a mutual agreement entered into between the Apostolic See and a State regarding matters which concern both parties, and is of the nature of a bilateral contract; cf. our *Summa Iuris Eccl. Publici*, 1910, p. 138 f.;

there is no reason to relinquish that notion.

4 Cfr. the saying: "*Ius quaesitum fortius est quam ius quaerendum.*" Cf. Barbosa, *Tractatus Varii*, Axioma 135, ed. Lugd. 1660, p. 89.

the triennial faculties. These remain unchanged unless
the Code expressly abolishes them, and consequently all
faculties obtained before the promulgation of the Code
and not expressly abolished therein remain in vigor until
they lapse.

CAN. 5

**Vigentes in praesens contra horum statuta canonum
consuetudines sive universales sive particulares, si
quidem ipsis canonibus expresse *reprobentur*, tanquam
iuris corruptelae corrigantur, licet sint immemorabiles,
neve sinantur in posterum reviviscere; aliae, quae
quidem centenariae sint et immemorabiles, tolerari
poterunt, si Ordinarii pro locorum ac personarum
adiunctis existiment eas prudenter submoveri non
posse; ceterae suppressae habeantur, nisi expresse Codex aliud caveat.**

Such customs, whether universal or particular,
as are now in vogue contrary to the prescriptions
of these canons, if they are expressly reprobated
by the canons, should be amended as corruptions
of the law, even though they be immemorial, and
should not be allowed to revive in future; others,
which are of century-long duration and immemor-
able, may be tolerated if the Ordinaries, with due
regard to places and persons, consider that they
cannot be prudently abolished; the rest shall be
regarded as suppressed, unless the Code expressly
provides otherwise.

On privileges and customs see *infra*, under the respective titles.

Can. 6

Codex vigentem huc usque disciplinam plerumque retinet, licet opportunas immutationes afferat. Itaque:

1.° Leges quaelibet, sive universales sive particulares, praescriptis huius Codicis oppositae, abrogantur, nisi de particularibus legibus aliud expresse caveatur;

2.° Canones qui ius vetus ex integro referunt, ex veteris iuris auctoritate, atque ideo ex receptis apud probatos auctores interpretationibus, sunt aestimandi;

3.° Canones qui ex parte tantum cum veteri iure congruunt, qua congruunt, ex iure antiquo aestimandi sunt; qua discrepant, sunt ex sua ipsorum sententia diiudicandi;

4.° In dubio num aliquid canonum praescriptum cum veteri iure discrepet, a veteri iure non est recedendum;

5.° Quod ad poenas attinet, quarum in Codice nulla fit mentio, spirituales sint vel temporales, medicinales vel, ut vocant, vindicativae, latae vel ferendae sententiae, eae tanquam abrogatae habeantur;

6.° Si qua ex ceteris disciplinaribus legibus, quae usque adhuc viguerunt, nec explicite nec implicite in Codice contineatur, ea vim omnem amisisse dicenda est, nisi in probatis liturgicis libris reperiatur, aut lex sit iuris divini sivi positivi sive naturalis.

The Code for the most part retains the discipline hitherto in force, but makes some opportune changes. Thus:

1.° All laws, whether universal or particular, that are opposed to the prescriptions of this Code, are abrogated, unless some special provision is made in favor of particular laws;

2.° Those canons which restate the ancient law without change, must be interpreted upon the authority of the ancient law, and therefore in the light of the teaching of approved authors;

3.° Those canons which agree with the ancient law only in part, must be interpreted in the light of the ancient law in so far as they agree with it, and in the light of their own wording in so far as they differ from the ancient law;

4.° When it is doubtful whether a canon contained in this Code differs from the ancient law, the ancient law must be upheld;

5.° As regards penalties not mentioned in the Code, whether spiritual or temporal, medicinal or (as they say) vindictive, whether incurred by the act itself or imposed by judicial sentence, they are to be considered as abrogated;

6.° If there be one among the other disciplinary laws hitherto in force, which is neither explicitly nor implicitly contained in this Code, it must be held to have lost all force unless it is found in approved liturgical books or unless it is of divine right, positive or natural.

This canon establishes the relation between the old and the new law of the Church, as explained in the Introduction to this Commentary, *supra*, pp. 60 sqq.

CAN. 7

Nomine Sedis Apostolicae vel Sanctae Sedis in hoc codice veniunt non solum Romanus Pontifex, sed

etiam, nisi ex natura rei vel sermonis contextu aliud appareat, Congregationes, Tribunalia, Officia, per quae idem Romanus Pontifex negotia Ecclesiae universalis expedire solet.

By the term " Apostolic See " or " Holy See " in this Code is meant not only the Roman Pontiff, but also, unless a different meaning follows from the nature of the thing or the context, the Congregations, Tribunals, and Offices by means of which the Roman Pontiff is wont to transact the affairs of the universal Church.

TITLE I

ON ECCLESIASTICAL LAWS

DEFINITION AND NATURE·

An ecclesiastical law may be defined as " a stable ordinance in accordance with reason, promulgated by the legitimate authority for the common welfare of the Church." [1] It is evident that a law spells stability and should always be based upon the dictates of reason, which requires that circumstances of person, ·time, and place should be duly considered.

Promulgation of ecclesiastical laws is necessary because, and in so far as, the will of the legislator must, in some way or other, be manifested to his subjects. [2]

The *mode of promulgation* depends on the legislator himself, and consequently is subject to change. Formerly ecclesiastical laws were promulgated in the City of Rome, at the gates of St. John Lateran, at St. Peter's, at the Apostolic Chancery and the Campo de' Fiori. The " Tametsi " had to be promulgated in every parish. Now an ecclesiastical law is sufficiently promulgated when it is published in the *Acta Apostolicae Sedis.*

CAN. 8

§ 1. **Leges instituuntur, cum promulgantur.**

[1] Accommodated from the definition of law in general by St. Thomas, *S. Theol.*, 1a 2ae, qu. 90, a. 4.

[2] It would be subversive of authority, as all canonists maintain (cf. the commentaries on tit. II Decretal.) to assert that the validity and obligatory force of laws depends on their acceptance by the people or clergy.

§ 2. **Lex non praesumitur personalis, sed territoria-lis, nisi aliud constet.**

§ 1. Laws go into effect when they are promulgated.

§ 2. A law is not presumed to be personal, but territorial, unless the contrary is evident.

CAN. 9

Leges ab Apostolica Sede latae promulgantur per editionem in *Actorum Apostolicae Sedis commentario officiali,* nisi in casibus particularibus alius promulgandi modus fuerit praescriptus; et vim suam exserunt tantum expletis tribus mensibus a die qui *Actorum* numero appositus est, nisi ex natura rei illico ligent aut in ipsa lege brevior vel longior vacatio specialiter et expresse fuerit statuta.

The laws enacted by the Apostolic See are promulgated by being published in the official *Acta Apostolicae Sedis,* unless some other mode of promulgation is prescribed in particular cases; and they become obligatory three months after the date affixed to the number of the *Acta* in which they appear, unless the nature of the law requires that it take effect immediately, or unless the law itself especially and expressly fixes a shorter or longer period.

Accordingly, a law published in the *Acta Apostolicae Sedis* bearing date of August 1, 1918, goes into effect at midnight Oct. 31 to Nov. 1, 1918.

CAN. 10

Leges respiciunt futura, non praeterita, nisi nominatim in eis de praeteritis caveatur.

Laws affect the future, not the past, unless it is expressly stated therein that they are retroactive.

A famous example of a retroactive law is the Constitution "*Consensus mutuus,*" of February 15, 1892, by which Leo XIII decreed that "henceforth in those places in which clandestine marriages are regarded as valid, all ecclesiastical judges who have cognizance of such matrimonial causes should forthwith cease to treat the intervention of carnal intercourse between betrothed persons as a presumption (*iuris et de iure*) of the marriage contract, and should not acknowledge or declare such union to be a lawful marriage." (Cfr. De Smet, *Betrothment and Marriage,* tr. by W. Dobell, Vol. II, Bruges, 1912, p. 18.)

LEGISLATORS IN THE CHURCH

Although the Code in its general rules does not mention the persons who are empowered to issue laws, it is safe to state that the following are ecclesiastical lawgivers:

1. The *Supreme Pontiff,* who in matters subject to ecclesiastical legislation may issue laws binding the whole Church. This he may do without or with his counsellors, through official organs, or personally.

2. The *Bishops* or Ordinaries, respectively, are entitled to issue laws for their respective territories. Their laws must be in conformity with the general laws or go beyond them; but without special commission or facul-

ties Bishops or Ordinaries are not empowered to issue laws *contrary* to the general law. Their legislative activity may be exercised either in synod or without.

3. *Superiors* of *communities* of *regulars* (with solemn vows), especially Generals, enjoy legislative power co-extensive with the power granted by the Supreme Pontiff and the Constitutions of their orders.

Other superiors of religious communities, if not exempt, cannot be said to possess legislative power, properly so called, although they may issue statutes and precepts.

OBLIGATION OF LAWS

In order to determine the obligatory force of a law, it must be noticed, as we have already stated, that a difference exists between divine (positive) and human laws. We may safely say that all moral laws which are based on the dictates of reason, have been laid down in Holy Writ. However, there are also positive divine laws which, *per se,* do not regulate the morality of acts, but determine the constitution of the Church and the Sacraments or the essentials of divine worship. These positive divine laws are out of the reach of human legislation and subject only to declaration or interpretation. They receive their obligatory force from divine law, natural and positive, and bind all the members of the Church without further injunction. Such laws evidently have no territoral limits. It is otherwise with *positive human laws,* which admit of distinction. Hence § 2 of Canon 8 (*supra*) says that a law must be presumed to be not personal but territorial, unless the contrary is evident, as, for instance, in case of the law prescribing the recital of the Breviary, which is manifestly personal.

Considering the *intrinsic* force of the obligation imposed by ecclesiastical law, we must make a distinction between merely prohibitive and nullifying laws. A merely *prohibitive* law renders an act against that law illicit, and this may be stated in barren terms, affecting merely conscience; or it may prohibit an act under penalty. In the former case we speak, with the old Roman jurisconsults, of a *lex minus quam perfecta*, in the latter of a *lex perfecta*, which has a penal sanction attached.

There is another species of laws, called *irritantes* or *inhabilitantes*, which are nothing else but *nullifying* laws, *viz.*, such as render an act committed contrary to them null and void (*lex plus quam perfecta*).

Now the Code says:

CAN. 11

Irritantes aut inhabilitantes eae tantum leges habendae sunt, quibus aut actum esse nullum aut inhabilem esse personam expresse vel aequivalenter statuitur.

Only those laws are to be considered as nullifying which state in express or equivalent terms that either the act is null and void or that a [certain] person is incapable [of performing a valid act against the law].

Thus, *e. g.*, the first degree of consanguinity renders a marriage null and void, whilst the attempted marriage of one *in sacris* is null by reason of the incapability of the person, expressly so declared. *Equivalent* means equal in force or significance so far as concerns the matter under consideration.

(Canons 12, 13, 14, and 15, *infra* pp. 86 sqq.)

The subject of nullifying laws is continued in Canon 15.

Can. 15

Leges, etiam irritantes et inhabilitantes, in dubio iuris non urgent; in dubio autem facti potest Ordinarius in eis dispensare, dummodo agatur de legibus in quibus Romanus Pontifex dispensare solet.

If a doubt arises as to the law, nullifying laws are not urgent; if there is a doubt regarding a fact, the Ordinary is empowered to grant a dispensation, provided there is a question of laws in which the Roman Pontiff is wont to dispense.

A *dubium juris* may arise from an imperfect knowledge of the existence of a law or its being in force. Such ignorance, of course, is not likely to be as common now as it was before the promulgation of the new Code. But even now, unless one is thoroughly acquainted with the law and the rules of interpretation, doubts may arise, without serious guilt, especially in cases or texts which refer to the old law.

A *dubium facti* may be caused by insufficient cognizance of a fact or its circumstances. Under this category falls, *e. g.*, the whole range of nullifying impediments. Ordinaries must acquaint themselves with the customs of the Roman Curia so as to know whether or not a dispensation may be granted in certain cases.

Can. 16

§ 1. **Nulla ignorantia legum irritantium aut inhabilitantium ab eisdem excusat, nisi aliud expressse dicatur.**

§ 2. **Ignorantia vel error circa legem aut poenam aut circa factum proprium aut circa factum alienum no-**

torium generatim non praesumitur; circa factum alienum non notorium praesumitur, donec contrarium probetur.

§ 1.   Ignorance of nullifying laws does not excuse from their observance, unless the contrary is expressly stated.

§ 2.   Ignorance or error concerning a law or a penalty or a fact which touches one's own person, or a notorious fact which touches another, as a general rule is not to be presumed; if, however, there is question of a fact regarding another, which is not notorious, ignorance or error may be presumed until the contrary has been established.

This canon does honor to the juridical sense of the law-framers against a certain tendency of minimizing the valor of laws.   A well known instance is that of the impediment of crime, which some authors wished to cover with the cloak of ignorance.

In regard to § 2 several observations are to be made:

a) *Ignorance* is the lack of necessary knowledge, whereas *error* is a state of mind approving falsehood for truth.   The former is negative, the latter positive and hence more obnoxious, but perhaps also less imputable.

b) A *notorious* fact is one which is publicly known and committed under circumstances that cannot be excused by any artifice (tergiversation) or aid of law (cf. can. 2197).

c) *Presumption* is anticipating a judgment, or forming a judgment from probable arguments and conjectures. Hence our Code defines presumption (a means of defence, but may here serve as a definition in law) as " a probable conjecture of a thing otherwise uncertain " (can. 1825). For " that which comes nearest to the proof of the fact is the proof of such circumstances as either necessarily or usually attend such facts; and these are called presumptions, which are only to be relied upon till the contrary be actually proved." [3] This is of particular service in matrimonial cases as also in the removal of pastors.

Who are *subject to the laws* of the Church?

CAN. 12

Legibus mere ecclesiasticis non tenentur qui baptismum non receperunt, nec baptizati qui sufficienti rationis usu non gaudent, nec qui, licet rationis usum assecuti, septimum aetatis annum nondum expleverunt, nisi aliud iure expresse caveatur.

Not bound by merely ecclesiastical laws are those who have not received Baptism, those who, though baptized, have not a sufficient use of reason, and those who, although they have attained the use of reason, have not yet completed their seventh year, unless the law expressly provides otherwise.

We shall deal with this canon *infra,* where we come to discuss the question who are subject to ecclesiastical laws.

The Code by mentioning *" merely ecclesiastical laws,"* intends to distinguish them from natural and divine (positive) laws as well as from those which, though

3 Cf. Blackstone-Cooley, Commentary, 1879, II, 371. It may be noticed that can. 1825 speaks of *praesumptio iuris* and *praesumptio hominis,* and of the former as *p. iuris simpliciter* and *p. juris et de jure;* here, however, presumption is taken in general, as referring to law,

formulated or more closely determined by human authority, are reductively called divine laws, *e. g.,* the threefold division of the clergy into bishops, priests, and ministers.[4] As examples of merely ecclesiastical laws we may mention irregularities, clearly determined penalties, etc., also the law of fasting and abstinence on certain days.[5]

The question may arise here, whether *baptized non-Catholics* are bound by merely ecclesiastical laws. As far as we can see the Code contains no explicit provision either pro or con, and hence the solution must be sought in the authorities on the old law. These generally agree that, *per se,* baptized non-Catholics are not exempt from the observance of ecclesiastical laws, because by Baptism a man becomes a member of the Church, although there may be, here and now, an obstacle preventing him from being an actual member.[6] The Church is not in a position to enforce these laws, but the right to do so is still radically inherent in the society established by Christ. If there should be a doubt as to the fact or validity of Baptism, the principle, *" in dubio favendum est libertati,"* may be applied. How careless Protestant sects, especially in large cities, are in regard to Baptism, is well known.

CAN. 13

§ 1. Legibus generalibus tenentur ubique terrarum omnes pro quibus latae sunt.

§ 2. Legibus conditis pro peculiari territorio ii subiiciuntur pro quibus latae sunt quique ibidem domi-

---

4 Can. 108, § 3 says *" ex divina institutione,"* and truly so, but the terminology was not settled until the beginning of the 2d century. Cfr. Bruders-Villa, *La Costituzione della Chiesa,* 1903, *passim.*

5 Lent is an ecclesiastical law, but to fast is a divine command. (Matth. IX, 15.)

6 Cfr. can. 87; Suarez, *De Leg.,* IV, 7, 2. A consequence is that Catholics should not offer flesh meat to Protestant servants on days of abstinence.

cilium vel quasi-domicilium habent et simul actu commorantur, firmo praescripto can. 14.

§ 1. General laws bind all for whom they are given, everywhere.

§ 2. Laws given for a particular territory bind only those for whom they are given and who have a domicile or quasi-domicile in that territory and actually reside therein, except as noted in Can. 14.

A general law (which term here appears to mean universal law) is one given for the entire Church and all its members, as, *e. g.,* yearly confession, hearing Mass, etc.

Particular laws are limited to the territory for which they are given, for instance, the law governing the election of bishops in the U. S., or laws made by provincial councils and diocesan synods. Particular laws suppose residence in the territory for which they are made,— residence conditioned by domicile, which the present canon limits to *domicile proper* and quasi-domicile. Domicile proper, according to the Roman law,[7] which has been adopted in this matter by canonists, is a fixed habitation in a certain place (municipality, parish) with the intention of staying there always. Hence actual residence, as manifested by the purchase or leasing of a house for an indefinite time, and the intention to remain in that place permanently, are signs of a true domicile. Now-a-days such fixed habitation is rare in large cities,

---

7 Cf. l. 7, *Cod. Iust.,* X, 10 de incolis: "habere domicilium non ambigitur, ubi quis larem (house-gods) rerumque ac fortunarum suarum summam constituit, unde rursus non sit discessurus, si nihil avocet, unde cum profectus est, peregrinari videtur; quodsi rediit, peregrinari jam destitit."

though frequent enough in farming districts. It is therefore entirely reasonable that a *quasi-domicile* should be admitted as meeting the requirements and order of law. This is established by actual residence in a certain parish or municipality with the intention of remaining there for the greater part of a year. This intention may be presumed if a person stays at least six months in the same place.[8] The distinction therefore between domicile and quasi-domicile consists in a difference of intention (*animus*), domicile requiring a perpetual, or at least an indefinitely protracted sojourn, whilst quasi-domicile may be established by a residence of six months. This quasi-domicile is acquired from the first day of residence if the person concerned can be proved to have had the intention of remaining there for the time stated.

This canon does not consider the monthly stay (can. 1097) peculiar to the matrimonial celebration.

The expression: *"For whom they are given"* (can. 13, § 1) calls for special attention. Laws given for laymen do not invariably apply to the clergy, and *vice versa*. Neither do all the laws intended for the secular clergy *eo ipso* bind the regular clergy; nor are the penal laws intended for the clergy meant for bishops and cardinals.

Some peculiarities are attached, by reason of laws being *per se* territorial, to foreigners (*peregrini*), *i. e.,* such persons as have for the moment relinquished their domicile or quasi-domicile, although they retain it (can. 91). Of these can. 14 treats as follows:

CAN. 14

§ 1. Peregrini:

1.° Non adstringuntur legibus particularibus sui territorii quandiu ab eo absunt, nisi aut earum trans-

8 Cf. Reiffenstuel, l. II, tit. 2, nn. 17 ff.

gressio in proprio territorio noceat, aut leges sint personales;

2.° Neque legibus territorii in quo versantur, iis exceptis quae ordini publico consulunt, vel actuum sollemnia determinant;

3.° At legibus generalibus tenentur, etiamsi hae suo in territorio non vigeant, minime vero si in loco in quo versantur non obligent.

§ 2. Vagi obligantur legibus tam generalibus quam particularibus quae vigent in loco in quo versantur.

§ 1. Strangers:

1.° Are not obliged to observe the particular laws of their own territory while they are absent therefrom, unless non-observance of these laws should prove detrimental in their own territory, or unless the laws are personal.

2.° Neither are they bound to observe the particular laws of the territory in which they are sojourning, with the exception of those that concern the public welfare or legal formalities.

3.° General laws they must observe, even though these laws are not enforced in their home territory; they are not bound to observe general laws if these laws are not binding in the place where they sojourn.

There is little to be said concerning the first clause. Some examples may illustrate the case. There is, e. g., the law binding every Catholic to support his pastor. If one is absent when the pew-rent is due, he is not, on account of his absence, free from the obligation of paying the same, because such an excuse would be detrimental to discipline. A bishop's obligation of applying Mass at stated times is incumbent on him even during his absence from the diocese, because it is personal.

The second clause concerns the particular laws of the territory in which one sojourns and provides that whatever is connected with the public welfare or concerns legal formalities, must be observed by strangers (*peregrini*).

The Code does not mention *scandal*, although canonists give that as a reason for the obligation of observing particular laws. The omission is probably due to the fact that scandal may negatively be reduced to considerations of public welfare. An instance may be taken from a particular diocesan statute concerning the frequenting of dramshops, which in some dioceses is forbidden under suspension, whilst in other dioceses no such sanction is attached.

Formalities (*sollemnia*) are outward details which must be observed in order to make an act legal. These are partly civil, *e. g.*, in contracts and last wills, and partly pertain to proceedings in the episcopal court.

The last clause, No. 3, touches upon general laws. An example may be furnished by the ten general holydays of obligation (can. 1247), of which only six are observed in the United States. An American travelling in countries where the ten holydays are kept, must observe them. A European, on the other hand, sojourning in this country, may conform himself to our custom.[9]

Section two added to our cannon concerns the *vagi, i. e.*, such as possess neither domicile nor quasi-domicile. They are obliged to observe both the general and the particular laws in effect at the place where they are staying. This regulation is somewhat stricter than usually ac-

---

9 A stricter view is taken by Suarez, *De Leg.* III, cc. 32 f.

cepted by commentators. Yet it is in keeping with the civil law and is really nothing else but the consistent application of the *forum competens*.[10]

INTERPRETATION OF LAWS

By interpretation we mean an explanation of the will of the legislator taken from the wording of the text. As the Roman emperors issued interpretations of obscure texts,[11] so did the popes, first and above all in matters of faith, but also, especially after authentic collections had been published, in disciplinary matters. The Council of Trent decreed that authentic interpretations should be given by the authority from which the law emanated. The S. C. Council was especially charged with interpreting the Tridentine decrees. Besides as the jurisconsults, too, rendered decisions or explanations, so did the canonists proffer their explanations, which at times were sought for, or at least accepted, by the Roman Court.

Thus we have a twofold interpretation, authentic and private. An *authentic* interpretation[12] proceeds from the maker of the law.

CAN. 17

§ 1. Leges authenticae interpretatur legislator eiusve successor et is cui potestas interpretandi fuerit ab eisdem commissa.

§ 2. Interpretatio authentica, per modum legis exhibita, eandem vim habet ac lex ipsa; et si verba legis in se certa declaret tantum, promulgatione non eget et valet retrorsum; si legem coarctet vel extendat aut

---

10 Cfr. c. 20, X, II, 2 de foro compet. and the commentators on the same, for instance, Reiffenstuel, II, 2, n. 44 f.; Engel, h. t., n. 11.

11 Blackstone-Cooley, *l. c.*, I, p. 58.

12 *Authentic* from the Greek αὐθέντης, means self-authorized, original, authoritative.

dubiam explicet, non retrotrahitur et debet promulgari.

§ 3. Data autem per modum sententiae iudicialis aut rescripti in re peculiari, vim legis non habet et ligat tantum personas atque afficit res pro quibus data est.

§ 1. Laws are authentically interpreted by the legislator or his successor, or by those to whom the power of interpretation has been given by either the legislator or his successor.

§ 2. An authentic interpretation, given in the form of a law, has the same force as the law itself; if it is merely a declaratory interpretation, it needs no promulgation and its obligatory force goes back to the day when the law itself was promulgated; but if the interpretation is restrictive or extensive or settles a doubt, it is not retroactive and requires to be promulgated.

§ 3. If an interpretation is given in the form of a legal judgment, or of a rescript in a special case, it has not the force of law, but binds only those persons and affects only those matters for whom or for which it is given.

As an authentic interpretation can be given only by the lawgiver or his successor and by those to whom the power of interpretation is committed by the lawgivers, the Pope and the Roman Curia (congregations, tribunals, offices) are the authentic interpreters of all those laws which proceed from the Sovereign Pontiff, whilst the Bishops or their successors are the interpreters of their own laws.

The interpreter may be in a position where he has either to extend the law or restrict it. He *extends* by interpretation if he applies the wording or text to cases or persons not mentioned in the law or not included in the original intention of the lawgiver, although the extension is not against the lawgiver's will;[13] for instance, exemption or papal enclosure to religious without solemn vows.[14]

A *restrictive* interpretation takes place when the law is limited to fewer persons or cases than the wording and the mind of the legislator would seem to indicate,[15] *e. g.*, if the people are interdicted but the clergy is not included. Besides doubts may arise, *e. g.* in rubrics, which must be solved. And, lastly, there may be required a merely *comprehensive* (declaratory) explanation, *viz.*, one which explains the law literally, but in more obvious terms, by substituting other words.

The Code (can. 17, § 2) says that an *authentic* interpretation of a law is of equal force with the law itself and has the same binding power; and if it be a merely declaratory interpretation, it needs no promulgation and its obligatory force goes back to the date of the promulgation of the law itself. An interpretation that is extensive or corrective (restrictive), on the other hand, must be promulgated and is not retroactive.

There is, however, another authentic interpretation possible, *viz.*, one demanded by parties directly interested. It may happen, for instance, that a matrimonial case, or a case of precedence, must be decided by way of interpretation. This is done by a so-called *judiciary interpretation*, rendered by a legitimate judge (can. 17, § 3). Evidently such an interpretation binds only the parties

13 Cfr. c. 3, 6°, III, 14.
14 Suarez, *l. c.*, VI, cc. 2 f.; Reiffenstuel, I, 2, n. 370 f.
15 Saurez, *l. c.*, VI, 5, 1: "Omnis restrictio legis eo tendit, ut mentem ipsam legislatoris ad pauciora coarctet, quam verba vel ratio legis prae se ferre videntur."

concerned and in the matter decided, and outsiders are not affected thereby.

Private interpretation, *viz.*, one given by jurisconsults not commissioned by the lawgiver, or by expert canonists (doctors), must be made in conformity with certain rules which are necessary for the right understanding of ecclesiastical — in fact of all — law. These rules are, of course, generally obeyed also by the authentic interpreters, but they are of importance especially in private interpretation and for those who wish to read and study Canon Law rightly. These rules are briefly the following:

CAN. 18

Leges ecclesiasticae intelligendae sunt secundum propriam verborum significationem in textu et contextu consideratam; quae si dubia et obscura manserit, ad locos Codicis parallelos, si qui sint, ad legis finem ac circumstantias et ad mentem legislatoris est recurrendum.

Ecclesiastical laws must be understood according to the proper meaning of the words considered in their context; if the meaning remains doubtful and obscure, recourse must be had to parallel texts in the Code, if there are any, to the purpose of the law and the circumstances surrounding it, and to the mind of the lawgiver.

Ecclesiastical laws must be interpreted in the light of their wording, as borne out by the context. Hither belong various rules culled from the Roman and the Canon Law: " Ubi verba non sunt ambigua, non est locus interpretationi; " [16] " Verba sunt intelligenda secundum

16 L. 25, Dig. 32 delegatis et fidei-com. (ed. Mommsen, 1902, p. 445).

propriam significationem," *i. e.*, in their usual and common signification;[17] " Verba generalia generaliter sunt sumenda," and " Ubi lex non distinguit, neque nos distinguere debemus."[18]

The *context,* too, must be considered, for it may be useful to compare words or sentences in the order and connection which they have with one another.

When the terms are *doubtful* and obscure, the interpreter must have recourse to parallel texts of the Code, and study the purpose and circumstances of the law and the mind of the legistator. Parallel texts are such as have an affinity with the subject or are expressly related to the same.   Here the rule holds good: " De similibus idem est judicium."[19] Note, however, that the similarity must bear on the point at issue.

The purpose or *end* of the law must be regarded in such a way that the interpretation really effects the scope, hence the rule: " Certum est, quod is committit in legem, qui legis verba complectens, contra legis nititur voluntatem." The scope is sometimes, especially in long decrees, premised in the preamble, which may then serve as a guide to the interpreter.

The *circumstances* surrounding a law are either *historical, i. e.,* facts which prompted the law, *e. g.,* the removal of a parish priest, or *real, i. e.,* actual needs and reasons of time and person.

The *mind of the legislator* must, of course, first and above all be deduced from the words of the law. Circumstances, context, subject, etc., also help to disclose the mind of the legislator, as well as the *ratio legis,* which is called the soul of the law. Hence the rule,

17 Reiffenstuel,   I,   2,   390   ff.;   18 Cf. Summarium ad l. 8, *Dig.,* 6,
Blackstone-Cooley, *l. c.,* I, p. 59.   2 de Publiciana.
    19 Cfr. can. 701 with can. 106; c. 2, X, I, 7; c. 3, X, I, 2.

"Non debet intentio verbis deservire, sed verba inten-
tioni." [20]

But we must guard against the assumption that the
intention of the interpreter may be carried into the
text. Hence if all the means so far enumerated fail in
discovering the true mind of the legislator, nothing is left
but to make direct inquiry by petitioning the competent
authority. Therefore we sometimes read: "Iuxta mentem," and the "mens" is set forth explicitly; but sometimes it must be guessed at, as said before.

Can. 19

**Leges quae poenam statuunt, aut liberum iurium
exercitium coarctant, aut exceptionem a lege continent,
strictae subsunt interpretationi.**

All penal laws as well as those which restrict
the free exercise of rights or embody an exception to the law, are subject to strict interpretation.

The first clause of this canon is contained in the well
known rule XV in Sexto: "Odia restringi, favores con-
venit ampliari," and rule 49, I. C.: "In poenis benignior
interpretatio est facienda." Such an interpretation is
neither extensive nor restrictive, but merely comprehensive; but an explanation which simply negatives the
penalty is no interpretation. Strict interpretation clings
to the text, and pays due regard to the mind of the legislator, but mitigates the rigor of the law as far as the *ratio
legis* will permit. What is meant by restricting the free
exercise of rights is best understood by the example of
the Ordinary exercising his rights as diocesan in appoint-
ments, etc.

Exceptions from laws may be either privileges or fa-

[20] Cfr. c. 11, C. 22, q. 5.

vors of a personal nature, or particular or special laws, which latter are called *exorbitantes*,[21] *i. e.*, running beyond the sphere of general or common law. For instance, a private oratory is a favor, exemption is a special law, and all these are subject to strict interpretation.

Can. 20

Si certa de re desit expressum praescriptum legis sive generalis sive particularis, norma sumenda est, nisi agatur de poenis applicandis, a legibus latis in similibus; a generalibus iuris principiis cum aequitate canonica servatis; a stylo et praxi Curiae Romanae; a communi constantique sententia doctorum.

If a general or a particular law contains no definite prescription concerning a case, unless there is question of applying a penalty, the rule for deciding such a case must be taken from laws given in similar cases, from the general principles of Canon Law based on equity, from the method and practice of the Roman Court, or from the common and constant teaching of approved canonists.

It is evident that a lawgiver cannot foresee or anticipate all the cases that may arise in practice in connection with his law. Hence something is always left to private judgment. Now there are four sources from which private judgment may draw aid in solving exceptional cases. They are:

1. The "usus forensis" or "auctoritas rerum similiter iudicatarum." This is nothing else but the norm of customary procedure and decisions previously rendered in

21 Cf. c. 11, C. 22, q. 5.

cases similar to the one in dispute. Although such decisions, especially if they have emanated from the Roman tribunals, must be received respectfully, and may be followed securely, yet their force does not extend so far as not to admit of a contrary verdict if the reasons are strong enough to upset former decisions.[22]

2. The second means of deciding cases is recourse to general legal principles based on the equity of Canon Law. That *equity* is a means of practical interpretation and application is evident, for reason dictates that, if a law is deficient in a particular case, it should be applied according to the principles of law, indeed, but with a human feeling.[23]

The principles, of course, must be taken from Canon, not from civil law. It is surprising that the Code does not refer to *civil laws* at all, except in so far as concordats are concerned. Hence in interpreting the Code it would be useless to refer to civil laws, and we merely note the fact that there is no palpable trace in the New Code of " canonized " civil laws, *i. e.*, civil laws formally sanctioned by the Church. On the other hand it is plain that just laws issued by the civil power are not spurned by the ecclesiastical authorities but accepted and proposed as binding the members of the Church.

3. The third means of applying the law is by rendering a decision in default of an existing law in accordance with the *stylus curiae*. From remote antiquity, as the " Liber Diurnus " [24] shows, the Roman Court or Apostolic Chancery employed a uniform, nay almost stereotyped mode of expediting affairs. This " stable method

22 Boekhn, *Comment. in Jus Universum,* 1735, I, 4, n. 39.

23 L. 8, *Cod. Iust.,* III, 1: " Placuit in omnibus rebus praecipuam esse iustitiae aequitatisque quam stricti iuris rationem; "— but this feeling must not be indulged too far, lest it destroy all law. Blackstone-Cooley, *l. c.,* I, p. 61.

24 Ed. Th. Sickel, 1889.

of proceeding in ecclesiastical causes and dispatching apostolic documents " is called the style of the Roman Curia. It partakes of the nature of a law for the different tribunals and the parties engaged in litigation before them.[25]

4. The last mode of propounding or expounding a case is the *authority of the school*. That the professional canonists have exerted a decided influence since the time of Gratian, not only upon decisions but on lawmaking itself, is well known. The " school " itself distinguished a threefold class of opinions: *communissima*, when all authors agreed; *communis*, when several weighty authors held the same opinion; *controversa*, when there was disagreement among canonists.[26] And it was always regarded as rash to deviate from the *opinio communissima*. The Code mentions the " common and constant opinion " of the school as a guiding principle in deciding a doubtful case, and justly so because such a consensus is sufficient for moral certainty. For the rest, even the *opinio communissima* does not constitute law.

Applying these rules, and especially that of equity, one may persuade himself that a certain law does not apply to himself under given circumstances. This may be true. However, since the law is intended for the common welfare, it is necessary to consider the rule laid down in canon 21.

CAN. 21

Leges latae ad praecavendum periculum generale, urgent, etiamsi in casu peculiari periculum non adsit.

Laws given in order to guard against a common

---

[25] Riganti, *Comment. in Reg. Canc. Ap.*, 45, § 1, n. 96.

[26] Schulte, *Quellen*, 1860, I, p. 258.

danger must be observed even if that danger in a particular case is absent.

The term *"generale"* here has reference to the community or body of the faithful, because a term extends to the species contained in the genus.[27] However, the term may also be taken as comprising a certain class of members, *e. g.,* the clergy, or the laity. Thus the law of reading forbidden books binds all, the law of guarding the *privilegium fori,* the clergy only, etc.

CESSATION OF LAWS

CAN. 22

Lex posterior, a competenti auctoritate lata, abrogat priori, si id expresse edicat, aut sit illi directe contraria, aut totam de integro ordinet legis prioris materiam; sed firmo praescripto can. 6, n. 1, lex generalis nullatenus derogat locorum specialium et personarum singularium statutis, nisi aliud in ipsa expresse caveatur.

A later law, given by competent authority, abrogates an earlier one if it expressly says so, or if it is directly contrary to it, or re-orders the subject-matter of the older law; however, Can. 6, No. 1 of this Code remains in full force, that is to say, a general law in no wise derogates from the laws in force in particular places or with regard to particular persons, unless the contrary is expressly provided therein.

27 Cf. Barbosa, *Tractatus Varii,* Axioma 106: "Generalis dispositio omnes species comprehendit." Suarez, *De Leg.,* III, c. 30. This is, of course, more urgent when there is necessity of professing the faith or maintaining its unity or obeying superiors.

In other words, an existing law loses its force if a new law is made by which it is abolished. This may be done (a) by an act of explicit abrogation, or (b) in virtue of the prescriptions of the new law being directly opposed to that of the old, or (c) if the new law reorders the entire subject-matter of the old.

a) Papal constitutions sometimes contain the clause, " hac immutabili et in perpetunm valitura constitutione." This is merely an emphatic assertion that the law should not be recalled without reason; it does not bind the Pope's successor, because " par in parem non habet imperium." [28] If the successor expressly mentions his predecessor's law as abolished, the latter loses its force.

b) A later lawgiver may issue a law about a matter (e. g. matrimonial) which runs contrary to former laws; hence the rule, " Lex posterior generalis derogat legi priori generali."

c) A thorough overhauling of the subject-matter has the same effect, for instance, in the removal of parish priests.

However, a general law does not abrogate a particular or special law unless the intention of the lawgiver is clearly expressed to that effect in a special clause. Such a clause would be, " non obstantibus quibuscunque etiam speciali vel specialissima mentione dignis." [29] In the canon quoted the Code ordains that all particular and special laws remain in force unless the contrary is expressly stated. Thus, e. g., the particular law on episcopal nominations in the U. S. remains in force even under the new Code.

CAN. 23

In dubio revocatio legis praeexsistentis non prae-

[28] Cfr. c. 20, X, I, 6 de elect.
[29] Cfr. the Constitution of Bene-
dict XV prefixed to the Code, *supra*, pp. 64 sqq.

sumitur, sed leges posteriores ad priores trahendae
sunt et his, quantum fieri possit, conciliandae.

Where there is doubt whether or not a law has
been revoked, [by the Code or by another general
law], it may not be presumed that the law has
been revoked, but the old law should be compared
with the new, and both made to harmonize, as far
as possible.

This canon expresses the law of continuity in the legislation of the Church. It would be unwarranted to as-
sume — as has, strangely enough, been done — that the
new Code came into being like a *Deus ex machina* and
that an insurmountable wall is now erected between the
Corpus Juris Canonici (in a wider sense) and the Code.
The sources (*fontes*) quoted will show the continuity of
legislation.

CAN. 24

Praecepta, singulis data, eos quibus dantur, ubique
urgent, sed iudicialiter urgeri nequeunt et cessant resoluto iure praecipientis, nisi per legitimum documentum
aut coram duobus testibus imposita fuerint.

Precepts given to individuals oblige those for
whom they are given, everywhere, but they cannot be juridically enforced, and cease to bind
when the lawgiver loses his authority, unless indeed they were imposed by a legal document or
in the presence of two witnesses.

A precept (command, injunction), therefore, differs
from a law, in as far as it " cleaves to the person to

whom it is given" (*ossibus inhaeret*) and ceases with
the authority or office of the one who gave it. Hence if
an Ordinary has given a precept [30] to a clergyman, that
precept does not bind after the death or resignation of
the Ordinary, unless the precept was given peremptorily
by way of an official document (not merely a paternal letter) or in the presence of two witnesses (examiners).

30 Cfr. for inst. can. 2177, against *concubinarii*.

TITLE II

CUSTOM [1]

Logically the Code now proceeds to deal with that other source of legal obligation known as Custom. Custom (*consuetudo*) generally speaking is a " law introduced by uniform and constant usage of the people with the consent of the legitimate power." Two elements, therefore, constitute the essence of a customary law: a *material* one, which consists of a certain number of repeated acts, and a *formal* one, which is the consent of the legislator. Canon 25 asserts that an ecclesiastical custom obtains its obligatory force solely from the consent of ecclesiastical authority.

CAN. 25

Consuetudo in Ecclesia vim legis a consensu competentis Superioris ecclesiastici unice obtinet.

An ecclesiastical custom derives legal force solely from the consent of the ecclesiastical superior.

The word *unice* in the text clearly refers to *consent*.

The Code wisely abstains from determining the nature of the consent required.

Consent may be *express*, *i. e.*, given by words or conclusive signs explicitly approving a custom; or *tacit*,

1 Cfr. title IV of the Decretals and the commentators thereon.

given by the fact that the lawgiver, though aware of the custom and in a condition to oppose it, does not contradict; or finally, *legal,* which is nothing else but the will of the legislator supposedly permitting a custom. The majority of canonists teach that *legal consent* suffices for introducing a custom.[2] The fact that customs have been introduced which the sovereign Pontiffs at first ignored[3] and afterwards accepted, seems abundant proof for that opinion.

That legal consent is *required* for the validity of a custom follows from the nature of the latter as a law; a law must proceed from legitimate authority.

As to the material element or *repeated acts,* these must bear the character of usage, and hence be frequent, public, and uniform. *Frequency* supposes more than one act, at least in common parlance. They must be *public* because they supply the formal act of promulgation; and *uniform* in order to demonstrate the conviction of the people.[4] This latter quality (uniformity) calls for another requisite, *viz., voluntariness.* The acts constituting a custom must be voluntary, for the people, in order to create or show the *persuasio juris,* must be free of intrinsic and extrinsic coercion,— in other words, they must not be under the impression as if they were bound to observe the custom in question because they falsely believe it to be a law.[5] Hence the intention of obliging themselves is necessarily included in the formation by the people of a custom.

One may ask, how can any one oblige himself to com-

---

2 Cfr. Reiffenstuel, I, 4, n. 136 ff.

3 Cfr. c. 2, 6°, I, 2: "Quia tamen locorum specialium et personarum singularium consuetudines potest probabiliter ignorare."

4 Cfr. c. 5, X, V, 41; Bockhn,

l. c., I, 4, nn. 31 ff.; Zallinger, *Iustit. Iuris Eccl.,* l. I, tit. 4, § 228 f.

5 Cfr. the glossa on c. 11, h. t.; v. Scherer, *l. c.,* I, p. 132.

mit a sin? This objection supposes the distinction between *a custom against the law* and *a custom beyond the law*.

A *custom against* the *law* (*contra legem*) does not create law, but merely removes the obligation of observing a law contrary to custom, whilst a custom *beyond* or *besides the law* constitutes a law in defect of a law (*deficiente lege inducit obligationem legis*). The latter alone is a custom properly speaking.[6] The objection stated supposes *mala fides* in those who commence a custom contrary to a law which they are supposed to know. We do not deny that those who first act against the law may be *in mala fide;* for they may act with a doubtful conscience, which is not permitted except under certain well-defined circumstances. However, we fairly deny that *mala fides* is always the first cause of acting against a law. There may be a thorough conviction that a law is no longer useful or adapted to circumstances, and hence had better be disregarded. Besides, it must be maintained that the people directly and reflexly have the will only of freeing themselves from a burden or restriction opposed to liberty, which reflexive will cannot be said to be evil in itself. Therefore *mala fides* must not necessarily be supposed; and even if it were present in the beginning, it may disappear afterwards. At any rate, a custom against a law may arise [7] either with or without *mala fides*. The next query may be: what is understood by *people,* for so far we have only spoken of the people in general. Canon 26 answers that question.

---

6 A custom according to law (*iuxta legem*) is strictly no custom at all, but simply a vivid expression and interpretation of an existing law; hence can. 29 says: "*consue- tudo optima legum interpres,*" which needs no comment.

7 Cf. Reiffenstuel, I, 4, nn. 142 ff.; Boekhn, I, 4, nn. 19 ff.; Wernz, *Ius Decretalium*, ed. 1, I, 255.

Can. 26

Communitas quae legis ecclesiasticae saltem recipiendae capax est, potest consuetudinem inducere quae vim legis obtineat.

A community which is capable of having an ecclesiastical law imposed on it, can introduce a custom which may obtain the force of law.

Law and custom suppose a certain amount of autonomy. This is verified in corporations acknowledged as such by the Church — for we are concerned with ecclesiastical law — and hence: (a) the Church at large, (b) ecclesiastical provinces and dioceses, and (c) ecclesiastical corporations specially designed as such, for instance, religious orders, also single exempt monasteries (e. g., of Benedictines), cathedral chapters, and congregations which enjoy exemption. Congregations of religious with simple vows, or rather, let us say, diocesan institutes, are incapable of introducing a custom, primarily so-called, because they lack autonomy in the proper sense. For the same reason ecclesiastical parishes cannot form a custom, although both parishes and diocesan institutes may have observances.[8]

Two other elements essential to custom are contained in canons 27 and 28.

Can. 27

§ 1. Iuri divino sive naturali sive positivo nulla consuetudo potest aliquatenus derogare; sed neque iuri ecclesiastico praeiudicium affert, nisi fuerit rationabilis et legitime per annos quadraginta continuos et comple-

---

8 Reiffenstuel, l. c., nn. 110 ff.

tos praescripta; contra legem vero ecclesiasticam quae clausulam contineat futuras consuetudines prohibentem, sola praescribere potest rationabilis consuetudo centenaria aut immemorabilis.

§ 2. Consuetudo quae in iure expresse reprobatur, non est rationabilis.

§ 1. No custom can in any wise derogate from a divine law, be it natural or positive; nor does any custom prejudice an ecclesiastical law, unless it is a reasonable custom and has obtained for forty continuous and full years; the only custom that can obtain against an ecclesiastical law containing a clause prohibiting future customs, is a reasonable custom that has existed for a century or from time immemorial.

§ 2. No custom is reasonable which is expressly reprobated by law.

If custom is a law which is essentially reasonable, the custom itself must be reasonable. Consequently no unreasonable custom is admissible. Canonists have laid down certain marks or notes by which a custom is shown to be unreasonable. A custom is unreasonable,

a) If it is contrary to natural and divine law or if it runs counter to faith and morals;[9]

b) If it is repugnant to the constitution of the Church, *e. g.*, if laymen would usurp ecclesiastical power,[10] if a council would set itself above the pope, if a priest would claim episcopal power, if the liberty of the Church were

9 Cc. 4, 8, 11, Dist. 12; cc. 8, 9, 10 C. 14, X, I, 6 de elect. X, V, 3 de simonia.

curtailed, or the free communication between pastor and faithful disturbed, etc.

c) If it is subversive of ecclesiastical discipline, for instance, contempt of censures,[11] multiplicity of benefices in the same hand,[12] and for religious communities if they should elect a superior from a different order.[13]

d) If a custom is reprobated by law.[14]

The other element is *prescription*,[15] which here means the time during which a custom has prevailed. Prescription, according to the Code, requires forty continuous and complete years. By this decision the Code has cut a Gordian knot and stopped much unnecessary waste of paper. The Code has gone even farther by demanding a centennial or immemorial prescription in cases where a custom is directed *against* an ecclesiastical law which contains a clause prohibiting future customs. For a custom *beyond* the law forty full years' prescription is also required.

CAN. 28

Consuetudo praeter legem, quae scienter a communitate cum animo se obligandi servata sit, legem inducit, si pariter fuerit rationabilis et legitime per annos quadraginta continuos et completos praescripta.

A custom beyond the law, which has been knowingly observed by a community with the intention of binding itself, becomes a law if it is

11 C. 5, X, I, 4: "insordescere in censuris."

12 C. 1, 6°, I, 4.

13 C. 1, Clem. I, 3.

14 Our Code employs the term "reprobata consuetudine" quite frequently.

15 Canonists of note reject prescription as a requisite for custom, but erroneously; cfr. Schulte, *Quellen*, I, p. 223 ff.; v. Scherer, I, 133.

reasonable and has been legitimately observed for forty full and continuous years.

Here we must revert to canon 5 (*supra*, p. 76) among the general norms, for it is directly connected with the present subject. This canon ordains, as we have seen, that all customs, either universal or particular, although immemorial, which are contrary to the canons here embodied and are expressly condemned as corruptions, must be set right nor be allowed to revive. Other customs, if centennial and immemorial, may be tolerated when the Ordinaries deem, according to circumstances of time and persons, that they cannot be abolished, while all other customs must be regarded as suppressed unless the Code provides otherwise. This canon states the relation of the customs in use at the time of the Code's going in force, *i. e.*, the 19th of May, 1918, to the canons of the new Code, but it also touches future customs. Customs which are expressly reprobated in the new Code (cfr. can. 818 etc.) must be abolished because the Church regards them as corruptions. The future is considered as far as it is incumbent upon Sion's watchmen to guard against revival.

The second clause of Canon 5 treats of customs which are *per se* reasonable but not in keeping with the new Code. Such customs, if centennial and immemorial, may be tolerated. There seems to be a difference between a centennial and an immemorial custom, because the former term denotes a precise duration, whereas the latter implies no more than a span of time that is beyond the memory of a fairly old person; for instance, two generations may suffice to accept an immemorial custom.[16]

---

[16] All commentators agree that "consuetudo immemorialis seu in- veterata sit illa cuius initii non ex- tat memoria." Cfr. c. 26, X, V, 40,

But canon 5 employs the conjunctive particle "*et*" (and), while canon 27, § 1, when speaking of prescription, employs the disjunctive particle "*aut*" (or). The difference lies in the introduction and abolition of customs, inasmuch as a legislator seems more ready to connive at the use of customs than at their opposition to a newly published code,— which position is entirely intelligible. However, all customs which are not of the venerable age indicated, should be suppressed, although common sense must even here have its sway; for common sense is based upon the dictates of reason and goes a long way.

CAN. 29

Consuetudo est optima legum interpres.

Custom is the best interpreter of laws.

This canon needs no further explanation in view of what we have said above.

ABOLITION OF CUSTOMS

CAN. 30

Firmo praescripto can. 5, consuetudo contra legem vel praeter legem per contrariam consuetudinem aut legem revocatur; sed, nisi expressam de iisdem mentionem fecerit, lex non revocat consuetudines centenarias aut immemorabiles, nec lex generalis consuetudines particulares.

Can. 5 remaining in full force, a custom either against or beyond the law may be revoked by a

to which the Gloss adds: "diligenter   sive privilegium inducit."
notandum quod consuetudo illa ius

contrary custom or law; however, a law, unless it makes express mention thereof, does not abolish centenary or immemorial customs, nor does a general law abolish particular customs.

That a contrary custom may make another custom ineffective, is evident; for custom is law, and therefore, as a law is revoked by a contrary law, so also a custom may be revoked by a contrary custom. Only we must notice that the contrary custom must fully cover the old custom and be vested with the requisites set forth above. As to the effect which a *contrary law* exerts upon a custom, the canon says that it does not revoke a custom unless it contains an express clause to that effect. Such *clauses* are: "*nulla obstante consuetudine,*" and "*nulla obstante consuetudine etiam immemoriali.*" The first clause revokes any general (not particular) custom less than centennial or immemorial; the second abolishes also immemorial customs. If the lawgiver wishes to do away with some particular custom, he adds the clause "*non obstante consuetudine etiam particulari*" or some similar expression. A custom expressly called "*reprobata*" is abolished even by the first-quoted simple clause.[17]

One last question: *Can a custom arise against the new Code itself?* The same query was made concerning customs arising against the decrees of the Council of Trent. Hence we answer with the majority of canonists:[18] A custom branded as reprobate, being unreasonable, cannot be admitted at all or only with greatest difficulty, but other customs may arise also against the new Code. For the resp. *clausulae* are nothing but disciplinary laws, and disciplinary laws admit of a contrary custom.

17 Cf. Reiffenstuel, I, 4, n. 190.   18 Cfr. Aichner, *l. c.,* § 17, 3.

TITLE III

ON THE RECKONING OF TIME

The present title does not deal with the chronology employed in papal documents, but with the canonical method of calculating time. It may be noted that since the pontificate of Gregory VII (1073–85) the reign of each pontiff commenced with his election, and papal documents were dated according to the year of the Incarnation (25 March) or Christmas Day. Now they are dated according to the calendar year. The indictions (periods of fifteen years) have also disappeared without detriment to chronology. This premised, we will now follow the Code in its determination of the value and duration of the different components of time.

CAN. 31

Salvis legibus liturgicis, tempus, nisi aliud expresse caveatur, supputetur ad normam canonum qui sequuntur.

Aside from the liturgical laws, time must be reckoned according to the norms established in the following canons, unless a different method is expressly provided.

The *liturgical norms* which are here excepted from the following rules, concern the liturgical year commencing with the first Sunday of Advent, the celebration of feastdays (*a vespera usque ad vesperam*), as far as the office is concerned, and the gaining of indulgences. In these matters then, which were noted in the *computus ecclesiasticus*, the Code does not make a change.[1]

CAN. 32

§ 1. Dies constat 24 horis continuo supputandis a media nocte, hebdomada 7 diebus.

§ 2. In iure nomine mensis venit spatium 30, anni vero spatium 365 dierum, nisi mensis et annus dicantur sumendi prout sunt in calendario.

§ 1. The day consists of twenty-four hours calculated from midnight; the week of seven days.

§ 2. The law reckons the month as a period of thirty days, the year as a period of 365 days, unless it is expressly declared that month and year are to be taken as they are in the calendar.

This is to be understood in the case only of several months or years being enumerated without any further designation, or in the sense of a period, where a month would equal 30 days, and *vice versa*.

CAN. 33

§ 1. In supputandis horis diei standum est communi loci usui; sed in privata Missae celebratione, in privata horarum canonicarum recitatione, in sacra communione recipienda et in ieiunii vel abstinentiae lege servanda, licet alia sit usualis loci supputatio, potest quis sequi

---

1 Cf. Gavanti, *Thesaurus S. Rituum*, Venet., 1740, II, 17 ff.; Van der Stappen, *Sacra Liturgia*, Mechl., 1898, I, 123 ff. Concerning indulgences S. O. (de indulg.), Jan. 26, 1911.

tempus aut locale sive verum sive medium, aut legale sive regionale sive aliud extraordinarium.

§ 2. Quod attinet ad tempus urgendi contractuum obligationes, servetur, nisi aliter expressa pactione conventum fuerit, praescriptum iuris civilis in territorio vigentis.

§ 1. In reckoning the hours of the day, the common local usage must be followed; but in the private celebration of Mass, in the private recitation of the Breviary, in receiving Holy Communion, and in the observance of fast and abstinence, though the usual computation of time differs, one may follow the local time, true or mean, or the legal time, regional or extraordinary.

§ 2. When there is question of enforcing contractual obligations, the time prescribed by civil law should be followed, unless otherwise expressly agreed upon.

Common usage reckons the day from midnight to midnight. In some countries twice twelve hours are counted, while in others (e. g., Italy) the watch shows twenty-four continuous hours. Some liberty is granted in the private celebration of Mass, the private recitation of the Breviary, receiving Holy Communion and observing the laws of fast and abstinence. In these matters one may follow local or legal custom, although both may differ from common usage. Local custom may have accepted the real or mean solar time, whilst legal custom is that assumed by law and acknowledged in a province or country. The astronomical calculation of a day would be that of sidereal time, which differs from the mean solar time, the solar day being some three minutes and fifty-five seconds longer than the sidereal day.[2] What is of practical use, however, is to know that in the United States there are five different kinds of time, 15° of longitude corresponding exactly to one hour of time difference. The time of the 60th meridian is called *Colonial,* that of the 75th Meridian, *Eastern,* that of the 90th, *Central,* that of the 105th, *Mountain,* that of the 120th, *Pacific time.*[3] In fulfilling the duties mentioned in the canon, one may follow sidereal time, if one is a good astronomer, or the mean solar time, generally called " railroad time."

In matters of *contract* the time assumed by civil law must be followed, unless otherwise agreed upon by the contracting parties. In this country the laws of the different States will, therefore, have to be consulted.[4]

The next canon enters into details which touch more closely upon the *starting and finishing point of a given period,* and a distinction is drawn between juridical and calendar time. It is well known that the English law, for instance, has a double way of counting time. Thus when a deed speaks of a month, it is a lunar month consisting of 28 days, unless the context shows that a calendar month of 31 days was intended. Thus also, according to English law, when a calendar month's notice of action is required, the day on which it is served is included and reckoned one of the days; and therefore, if a notice be served on the 28th of April, it expires on the 27th of May, and the action may be commenced on

2 Cfr. Young, *Manual of Astronomy,* 1902, p. 84 ff.
3 Cfr. the *New International Encycl.,* 1904, Vol. XIX, p. 291.
4 Cfr. Blackstone-Cooley, *l. c.,* II, p. 141 f.

the 28th. The same law, however, in ecclesiastical matters calculates the month according to the calendar or solar reckoning.[5] This premised, let us see what the Code determines:

CAN. 34

§ 1. Si mensis et annus designentur proprio nomine vel aequivalenter, ex. gr., *mense februario, anno proxime futuro,* sumantur prout sunt in calendario.

§ 2. Si terminus *a quo* nec explicite nec implicite assignetur, ex. gr., *suspensio a Missae celebratione per mensem aut duos annos, tres in anno vacationum menses,* etc., tempus supputetur de momento ad momentum; et si tempus sit continuum, ut in allato primo exemplo, menses et anni sumantur prout sunt in calendario; si intermissum, hebdomada intelligatur 7 dierum, mensis 30, annus 365.

§ 3. Si tempus constet uno vel pluribus mensibus aut annis, una vel pluribus hebdomadibus aut tandem pluribus diebus, et terminus *a quo* explicite vel implicite assignetur:

1.° Menses et anni sumantur prout sunt in calendario;

2.° Si terminus *a quo* coincidat cum initio diei, ex. gr., *duo vacationum menses a die 15 augusti,* primus dies ad explendam numerationem computetur et tempus finiatur incipiente ultimo die eiusdem numeri;

3.° Si terminus *a quo* non coincidat cum initio diei, ex. gr., *decimus quartus aetatis annus, annus novitiatus, octiduum a vacatione sedis episcopalis, decendium ad appellandum,* etc., primus dies ne computetur et tempus finiatur expleto ultimo die eiusdem numeri;

4.° Quod si mensis die eiusdem numeri careat, ex.

5 Cfr. Blackstone-Cooley, I, p. 141.

gr., *unus mensis a die 30 Ianuarii*, tunc pro diverso casu tempus finiatur incipiente vel expleto ultimo die mensis;

5.° Si agatur de actibus eiusdem generis statis temporibus renovandis, ex. gr., *triennium ad professionem perpetuam post temporariam, triennium aliudve temporis spatium ad electionem renovandam*, etc., tempus finitur eodem recurrente die quo incepit, sed novus actus per integrum eundem diem poni potest.

On account of the technical character of this canon, we shall add our explanation immediately to each paragraph.

1. If months and years are designated by their names, or in equivalent terms, they must be understood as calendar months and years. Thus the month of February must be taken as comprising 28 days; if an equivalent term is used, as, *e. g.,* " in the next following year," let us say 1920, the leap year is understood, or 366 days, while the uneven years have each but 365 days.

2. If the starting point or *date from which* anything is calculated, is neither *explicitly nor implicitly determined,*[6] the time must be reckoned from moment to moment, thus, *e. g.,* a suspension from the celebration of Mass for a month or two years commences on the day and hour when the letter was received by the suspended priest. The same holds good concerning the other example alleged, *viz.,* three months' vacation a year. The canon further explains the first example thus: if the time or period is *continuous* (as in the case of suspension), the calendar month and year are to be understood; hence

---

6 Implicitly, for instance, after Easter Sunday, or on the feast of Pentecost, next month.

if the letter of suspension arrives at 5 P. M., let us say, on the 5th of October, the suspension lasts until December 5th, 5 P. M. If the time or period is or may be *interrupted,* as in the example of leave of absence, a week means 7 days, a month 30 days, a year 365 days.

3. If the time or period consists of one or more months, or years, or of one or more weeks, or of several days, and the starting point is *explicitly* or *implicitly determined,* various hypotheses may arise.

1°. Months and years are always assumed to be calendar ones.

2°. If the starting point (*terminus a quo*) *coincides* with the beginning of the day, the first is included in reckoning the time, and the time or period expires with the beginning of the last day of the same number, *e. g.,* if a two months' vacation is given, beginning August 15th, the time runs out on the morning of October 15th.

3°. If the starting point *does not coincide* with the beginning of the day, the first day is counted in and the term expires when the last day of the same figure is completed. Thus, if one commences a year's novitiate on the afternoon, say of the 5th of October, 1917, he can make his profession on October 6th, 1918, because the last day is complete only after the last stroke of midnight, October 5th, or as soon as October 6th has commenced.

4°. If the month has no day of the same number, say one month from January 30th, then, duly considering diverse cases, the term expires either with the beginning or ending of the last day. What "due consideration" means is evident from the two foregoing hypotheses; wherefore in the first case the month from January 30th is the 28th or 29th of February in leap years, if the *terminus a quo* fell on the beginning of the day; it ends on March 1st, if the *terminus a quo* fell on a later part of the day.

Here the difficulty may be mooted as to what is understood by the *beginning of a day*. The Code (can. 32) merely says that the days must be completed from midnight. Civil law, generally speaking, rejects fractions of a day.[7] Canon law, by enjoining computation " from moment to moment," if nothing is said to the contrary, considers fractions.[8] Hence, speaking of the beginning of a day (*initium diei*), the law means that part which, according to common usage, forms the first portion of the day. How far that can be stretched, is mere guesswork; but to extend it to noon would, in our opinion, be against the intention of the law as well as contrary to common usage. Nine o'clock would be about the limit.

5°. If a *recurrence of the same act* at stated times is in question, the term expires on the same recurring day, but the new act may be performed throughout the whole recurring day, for instance, profession after a term of three years, temporary vows, triennial elections, for instance, October 5th, 1917 — October 5th, 1920.

CAN. 35

Tempus *utile* illud intelligitur quod pro exercitio aut prosecutione sui iuris ita alicui competit ut ignoranti aut agere non valenti non currat; *continuum,* quod nullam patitur interruptionem.

The *tempus utile* is the time granted for exercising or prosecuting certain rights, so that in case one should ignore it or be unable to make use of it, the lapse of time would not damage or

---

7 Blackstone-Cooley, *l. c.,* p. 141.   8 Reiffenstuel, II, 27, n. 111.

prevent him; the *tempus continuum* is that which runs without interruption.

The so-called *tempus utile* is distinguished from the *tempus continuum*, *i. e.*, time which runs continually without regard to ferial days or the presence or absence of persons, etc. For instance, if the *tempus utile* for a *restitutio in integrum* were four years, and one were not aware of having been wronged, the time would not commence with the day of the wrongdoing but with the day when the defendant realized that action must begin;[1] thus also in cases of summons or citations.

1 Cfr. Engel, I, 41, n. 11 de in integrum restitutione.

TITLE IV

ON RESCRIPTS

A rescript is a written answer given by a legitimate ecclesiastical superior, either directly, or indirectly through the medium of a competent tribunal, to a question proposed or a favor asked for. As we have stated above, as early as the eleventh century there were two kinds of papal letters, *litterae gratiae* and *litterae justitiae*. *Litterae gratiae* or rescripts of favor proceed from the mere liberality — although perhaps petitioned — of the pontiff or bishop in matters wholly subject to their good pleasure and uncontested, *e. g.*, a nomination to a domestic prelacy. *Litterae justitiae* refer to justiciable matter to be settled between contending parties in legal form, *e. g.*, boundary disputes, questions of precedence, etc.

The definition says that rescripts may be granted directly or indirectly. To understand the difference between the two species note the fact that, as a general rule, the Pope issues rescripts through the ordinary Roman tribunals; yet he is not bound to use that means (can. 38).

Besides, it has become customary to send rescripts granted by the Roman Curia to an *executor*. The executor, as a rule, is a dignitary, *i. e.*, one constituted in a real or honorary dignity, most commonly the Ordinary of the diocese or, for religious, the superior general or provincial. There is a distinction between the *executor voluntarius* and the *executor necessarius;* the former acts as a judge, *i. e.,* he decides whether or not the rescript can be put into effect (can. 54); whereas the *executor necessarius* is obliged to sign and deliver the rescript to the person concerned. Whether an executor is *voluntarius* or *necessarius* depends on the clauses added to the rescript. If the conditional particles "*si*" or "*dummodo*" are to be found in the rescript, the executor is considered *voluntarius*, not a mere instrument for executing the will of the superior,[2] and hence is obliged to proceed as if he had received a *mandate* or authoritative commission, by which jurisdiction is given to him in the case (can. 55). These preliminary notions supposed, the Code first establishes *who are capable of demanding* a rescript, either from the Apostolic See or the Ordinaries, and lays down the rule that all may petition for a rescript, unless expressly incapacited under the law.

CAN. 36

§ 1. Rescripta tum Sedis Apostolicae tum aliorum Ordinariorum impetrari libere possunt ab omnibus qui expresse non prohibentur.

§ 2. Gratiae et dispensationes omne genus a Sede Apostolica concessae etiam censura irretitis validae sunt, salvo praescripto can. 2265, § 2, 2275, n. 3, 2283.

§ 1. Rescripts may be freely asked both from the Apostolic See and from other Ordinaries by all who are not expressly prohibited (from asking for them).

2 Sometimes an *exsecutor mixtus* is inserted between the two mentioned. An *exsecutor mixtus* is one who is authorized to execute *a gratia facienda*, which is a favor granted and only needs execution; this kind of executorship may be called a "*nudum ministerium.*"

§ 2. Favors and dispensations of all kinds granted by the Holy See are valid, even if the beneficiaries are under censure, with due regard, however, to can. 2265, § 2, can. 2275, n. 3, and can. 2283.

Favors and dispensations of all kinds granted by the Holy See even to censured persons are valid, *exceptis excipiendis*. The law *prohibits* the following from asking for a rescript: All *excommunicated* persons, which heading includes all heretics,[a] all those excommunicated after a declaratory or condemnatory sentence, and all who are personally interdicted or suspended, unless the rescript mentions the fact of excommunication. This is frequently done by the addition of the clause, "*absolutis a censuris,*" etc., which has no other effect than to render the petitioner capable of receiving the rescript; hence *de facto* he is not absolved from excommunication.

It must be furthermore noted that, according to all authors, even excommunicated persons are allowed to ask for a rescript revoking their excommunication, interdict, suspension, etc., else the way of justice would be precluded to them.

CAN. 37

Rescriptum impetrari potest pro alio etiam praeter eius assensum; et licet ipse possit gratia per rescriptum concessa non uti, rescriptum tamen valet ante eius acceptationem, nisi aliud ex appositis clausulis appareat.

A rescript may be obtained for another (or

[a] Cfr. c. 13, X, V, 7 de haereticis.

third) person even without the latter's consent; and though this third person may not be able to avail himself of the favor conceded by the rescript, yet the rescript is valid before its acceptance, unless otherwise provided for in the appended clauses.

The wording of this canon is not entirely clear; but comparing it with c. 28, X, I, 3, § 1, we may conclude that not only rescripts of favor, as the Decretals (l. c.) state, but also rescripts of justice, *i. e.,* all kinds of rescripts, are valid before the act of acceptance is made by the party unable (*e. g.,* because a heretic) to profit by the rescript.

The "appended clauses" may regard either the capability of the third person or the acceptation, which may be conditioned by circumstances of absence or other impediments.

DATE AND REQUISITES

CAN. 38

Rescripta quibus gratia conceditur sine interiecto exsecutore, effectum habent a momento quo datae sunt litterae; cetera a tempore exsecutionis.

Rescripts by which a favor is granted without the agency of an executor, take effect from the date of their signature; all others, from the date of execution.

Hence, *e. g.,* a rescript granting a personal or, generally speaking, a private favor is valid as soon as the Pope has signed it. All other rescripts take effect from the date of the executor's signature.

What about a *telephone* or *telegraph* message? Leaving aside matrimonial and other weighty matters, the telephone or telegraph may be used in order to transmit notice whether the petition was granted or not. It is certain that the Papal Secretary of State may use this means. Generally speaking, the person from whom notice is demanded must be an official who is in a position to know. Private persons are not to be relied upon.

According to Canon 56 (*infra*, p. 145) the rescripts which are handed over to an executor demand execution *in writing* if they regard the *forum externum*. However, after the executor has properly investigated the matter and signed the document, he may, if asked for, transmit an answer by telephone or telegraph and send the written document afterwards. Note, however, that such a transmission is the exception, not the rule.[4]

The Code insists on written execution only for those rescripts which do not directly concern the conscience, and hence those touching the *forum conscientiae* may be transmitted by these " extraordinary " means, provided, of course the *sigillum confessionis* is safeguarded.

CAN. 39

Conditiones in rescriptis tunc tantum essentiales pro eorundem validitate censentur, cum per particulas *si*, *dummodo*, vel aliam eiusdem significationis exprimuntur.

Conditions made in rescripts are essential to their validity only if they are expressed by the

---

4 The Secretariate of State, 10 Dec., 1891, has declared this kind of transmission an extraordinary one.

Cfr. De Smedt, *De Spons. et Mat.*, 1910, I, p. 532, p. 547.

particles *si, dummodo,* or others of the same meaning.

In omnibus rescriptis subintelligenda est, etsi non expressa, conditio: *Si preces veritate nitantur,* **salvo praescripto can. 45, 1054.**

In all rescripts, even when not expressly stated, this condition must be understood: *If the request is founded on truth,* with due regard to can. 45 and 1054.

Phrases of similar meaning as *si* and *dummodo* are the ablative absolute, *e. g.* "*constito de assertis*" or "*narratis,*" which is truly a conditional clause, so that if it were not verified the rescript would be invalid.[5] This condition, "*si preces veritate innitantur,*" is implied in every rescript, with the exception of "*motu proprio,*" with some modifications (see below). The reasons for a petition, and consequently for the validity of the grant, must actually exist at the time the rescript is signed by the grantor, provided no executor is assigned; if an executor is selected, the reason must be verified at the time when the executor signs the document. For instance, a rescript permitting a private oratory is valid when all the conditions for such an oratory are fulfilled at the date when the Ordinary (to whom such rescripts are generally directed) signs the paper. This is the meaning of Can. 41.

In rescriptis quorum nullus est exsecutor, preces

5 Cf. Barbosa, *Tractatus Varii,* de clausulis, n. 25, p. 375.

veritate nitantur oportet tempore quo rescriptum
datum est; in ceteris tempore exsecutionis.

In rescripts for which no executor is appointed,
the conditions upon which the petition is based
must be real at the time the rescript is signed; in
all others, at the time of the execution.

It may happen, however, that the grantor, and perhaps the executor also, were deceived by the petitioner,
who either did not state the full truth (*subreptio*) or alleged a reason which had no foundation in fact
(*obreptio*). Such a deception may arise either from
ignorance or malice.[8]   This difference is not mentioned in
the Code, which simply says:

Can. 42

§1. Reticentia veri, seu subreptio, in precibus non
obstat quominus rescriptum vim habeat ratumque sit,
dummodo expressa fuerint quae de stylo Curiae sunt
ad validitatem exprimenda.

§ 2. Nec obstat expositio falsi, seu obreptio, dummodo vel unica causa proposita vel ex pluribus pro-
positis una saltem motiva vera sit.

§ 3. Vitium obreptionis vel subreptionis in una tantum parte rescripti aliam non infirmat, si una simul
plures gratiae per rescriptum concedantur.

§ I.   Failure to state the full truth (*subreptio*)
in the petition does not prevent a rescript from
being valid and going into effect, provided men-

---

[8] Cfr. c. 20, X, I, 3, which chapter is called in the summary the "key of the whole title"; our canon dis- regards the distinction between *igno-rance* and *malice*.

tion was made of whatever the *stylus Curiae* requires for validity.

§ 2. Neither is a rescript obtained by the allegation of a falsehood (*obreptio*) invalid, provided the sole reason, or at least one of the several reasons alleged, is true.

§ 3. Either defect, *obreptio* or *subreptio*, occurring in only one part of a rescript, does not invalidate the other parts, if several favors are granted simultaneously by the same rescript.

As to the first clause (§ 1), the *stylus Curiae* prescribes certain canonical reasons for matrimony, the different lines and degrees, as well as certain formularies to be used in obtaining faculties or dispensations from the various Roman Congregations. This customary style is, of course, best known to the agents engaged in business with these Congregations. If a *petition* is not properly drawn up, it is usually *returned to the petitioner*, to be corrected.[7]

As to § 2: The *motive cause* or final reason (can. 45) is the one which moves the superior to grant a petition. If, therefore, this one is false, the rescript will be null and void, and the petitioner can neither licitly nor validly use the favor granted therein.

Note that our canon makes a distinction in favor of *subreptio*, which the Corpus Juris did not admit under the circumstance of deliberate falsehood, either expressed or suppressed.[8] The new Code is also benign in admitting the *divisibility of a rescript* which contains sev-

7 The *stylus Curiae* has been described above; cfr. also Putzer, *Comment. in Facultates Apost.*, 1897, p. 15. The *clausulae* also belong to the "Roman Style."

8 Cfr. c. 20, X, I, 3.

eral favors, *e. g.*, that of saying *de requiem* and reciting other prayers instead of the Breviary.

To provide for a uniform procedure and to avoid confusion, as well as to prevent rescripts from being, as it were, received stealthily, the following two canons have been inserted:

CAN. 43

Gratia ab una Sacra Congregatione vel Officio Romanae Curiae denegata, invalide ab alia Sacra Congregatione vel Officio aut a loci Ordinario, etsi potestatem habente, conceditur sine assensu Sacrae Congregationis vel Officii quocum vel quibuscum agi coeptum fuit, salvo iure S. Poenitentiariae pro foro interno.

A favor denied by one Sacred Congregation or Office of the Roman Curia cannot validly be granted by another Congregation or Office, or by the local Ordinary, even though he have the power, except with the consent of the S. Congregation or Office which handled the case first,—without, however, violating the right of the S. Penitentiary in matters of conscience.

CAN. 44

§ 1. Nemo gratiam a proprio Ordinario denegatam ab alio Ordinario petat, nulla facta denegationis mentione; facta autem mentione, Ordinarius gratiam ne concedat, nisi habitis a priore Ordinario denegationis rationibus.

§ 2. Gratia a Vicario Generali denegata et postea, nulla facta huius denegationis mentione, ab Episcopo impetrata, invalida est; gratia autem ab Episcopo

denegata nequit valide, etiam facta denegationis mentione, a Vicario Generali, non consentiente Episcopo, impetrari.

§ 1. No one shall ask another Ordinary for a favor refused by his own Ordinary without making mention of the refusal; if mention is made, the second Ordinary shall not grant the favor until informed of the reasons for the former Ordinary's refusal.

§ 2. A favor denied by the Vicar General and later obtained from the Bishop, without mention of the refusal, is invalid; a favor denied by the Bishop cannot validly be asked of the Vicar General without the Bishop's consent, even if mention of the refusal is made.

The underlying principle of this regulation is that the Roman Curia, as well as the Bishop and his Vicar General form a unit. Two different Bishops constitute two separate tribunals, wherefore in § 1 of Can. 44 the invalidity of the rescripts is not asserted,[9] but merely their illicitness, for the purpose touched above.

THE CLAUSE " MOTU PROPRIO "

Boniface VIII made a distinction between a rescript given " Motu proprio," which, he says, proceeds from pure liberality, and one obtained by petition.[10] In course of time, especially since Innocent VIII, " Motu proprios " became more frequent and were no longer acts of grace,

9 The "novum genus mercimonii" mentioned in c. 28, h. t., is thereby precluded.

10 Cf. c. 23, 6°, III, 4 de praebendis.

but could be petitioned for (*ad instantiam*) ; the Supreme Pontiff merely added "Motu proprio" in order to give full and unlimited effect. The new Code has partly retained this custom and partly modified it, as follows:

CAN. 45

Cum rescriptis ad preces alicuius impetratis apponitur clausula: *Motu proprio,* **valent quidem ea, si in precibus reticeatur veritas alioquin necessario exprimenda, non tamen si falsa causa finalis eaque unica proponatur, salvo praescripto can. 1054.**

Rescripts issued with the clause *Motu proprio* are valid, even if subreptitious, unless the final reason, if it be the only one, is falsely alleged.

For instance, if a rescript were obtained dispensing the petitioner from reciting the Breviary on account of weak eyes, and this claim rested on mere imagination, the rescript would be invalid. There are three other cases in which a " Motu proprio " is of no effect:

CAN. 46

Rescripta etiam *Motu proprio* **concessa personae de iure communi inhabili ad consequendam gratiam de qua agitur, itemque edita contra alicuius loci legitimam consuetudinem vel statutum peculiare, vel contra ius alteri iam quaesitum, non sustinentur, nisi expressa derogatoria clausula rescripto apponatur.**

A rescript, even though granted *Motu proprio,* is of no effect if given to a person incapable of the favor granted under the common law, or against the lawful custom or particular statute of the place, or against the acquired right of another person, unless a derogatory clause is appended to the rescript.

A rescript is invalid if given to a person who is incapable of the favor [11] granted because the law itself makes him incapable. The superior is not supposed to contradict the law. A favor is equally invalid if given against the lawful custom or a particular statute of the place or if it trenches on the lawfully acquired right of a third person. The reason for the last two provisions is the ignorance of a superior concerning particular laws and the *jura tertii*, which he is not supposed to infringe upon.[12] However, if a derogatory clause is appended directly affecting the incapability of the person, or particular laws, or the *jus tertii*, the rescript is valid. Exception is made in favor of matrimonial dispensations from minor impediments; see can. 1054.

MISTAKES IN RESCRIPTS

CAN. 47

Rescripta non fiunt irrita ob errorem in nomine personae cui vel a qua conceduntur, aut loci in quo ipsa moratur, aut rei de qua agitur, dummodo, iudicio Ordinarii, nulla sit de ipsa persona vel re dubitatio.

Errors affecting the name of the person to whom or by whom a rescript is issued, or the place where the person dwells,[13] or the favor itself, do

---

[11] For instance, if the petitioner suffers from irregularity, defect of age, illegitimate birth. Reiffenstuel, I, 3, n. 208 f. Of course, if the rescript is issued precisely to take away these defects, the petitioner becomes capable of the favor and consequently of the rescript.

[12] Cfr. c. 8, 6°, I, 3.

[13] However, a mistake about the diocese would invalidate the rescript. Cfr. c. 34, X, I, 3.

not render a rescript invalid, if the Ordinary is persuaded that no doubt exists as to the identity of the person or the thing asked for.

We may add, however, that as formerly, so now, a manifest error or an erasure in the dispositive and essential part would cast serious suspicion upon the genuineness of a papal document.[14]

PREFERENCE, INTERPRETATION, AND PRESENTATION

If several rescripts were obtained about one and the same question or subject-matter, e. g., some point of rubrics, let us say the recital of old or new canticles,[15] one rescript contradicting the other, the question arises, which one must be followed? The Code answers as follows:

CAN. 48

§ 1. Si contingat ut de una eademque re duo rescripta inter se contraria impetrentur, peculiare, in iis quae peculiariter exprimuntur, praevalet generali.

§ 2. Si sint aeque peculiaria aut generalia, prius tempore praevalet posteriori, nisi in altero fiat expressa mentio de priore, aut nisi prior impetratur dolo vel notabili negligentia suo rescripto usus non fuerit.

§ 3. Quod si eodem die fuerint concessa nec liqueat uter prior impetraverit, utrumque irritum est, et, si res ferat, rursus ad eum qui rescripta dedit, est recurrendum.

§ 1. If it should happen that two rescripts re-

---

[14] C. 11, X, I, 3; c. 6, X, II, 22 de fide instrumentorum.

[15] This happened in the Swiss-American Congregation of the Benedictine Order concerning a decree of June 9, 1915, and a rescript of later date; but the mistake was made in Rome.

ferring to the same matter are contradictory, the rescript containing a peculiar or particular enactment must be accepted in preference to the one containing a general enactment.

§ 2. If both rescripts are alike particular or general, the one which is dated or received earlier must be preferred to that of later date, unless specific mention is made in the latter rescript of the earlier one, or unless the first petitioner, through fraud or notable negligence, has not made use of the earlier rescript.

§ 3. If the two rescripts were issued on the same day, and it is not apparent which was obtained first, both are invalid, and, if feasible, recourse must be had to the grantor.

According to § 1, a special favor is to be preferred to a general one, because " species derogat generi." [16]

Fraud may be committed by withholding the document, and notable negligence would be failure to make use of the favor granted for one year.[17]

CAN. 49

Rescripta intelligenda sunt secundum propriam verborum significationem et communem loquendi usum, nec debent ad casus alios praeter expressos extendi.

Rescripts must be interpreted according to the proper meaning of the words and common par-

[16] Reg. juris 34 in 6°.
[17] Cf. cc. 9, 23, X, I, 3. Fraud is possible in marriage rescripts, but especially in rescripts of justice.

lance, nor are they to be extended to cases not mentioned therein.[18]

Four kinds of rescripts must be interpreted *strictly*, *i. e.*, neither extensively nor restrictively, but according to the exact wording of the text, to wit: (a) rescripts of justice which are intended to settle a controversy; (b) those which may injure the acquired rights of others; (c) those which are adverse to the special laws of private persons; and (d) those which contain an appointment to an ecclesiastical benefice. All other rescripts may be broadly and benignly interpreted; *"favores ampliandi sunt."* The reason for interpreting the first kind strictly is that the superior wishes to prevent litigation and this object could not be accomplished if a broad interpretation were admissible.[19] The reason for interpreting the second and third kind of rescripts strictly must be sought in the intention of the superior of defending the rights of others, especially if these are acquired by privileges, *e. g.*, of exempt religious. The reason for a strict interpretation of rescripts in beneficiary matters lies in the fact that such rescripts favor ambition. Hence if, *e. g.*, a dignity or office in a cathedral chapter is conferred, the two are not to be taken promiscuously. All other rescripts of favor are susceptible of a broad interpretation, because *"plenissima alias in beneficiis interpretatio facienda."* [20]

As to *presentation*, which is nothing else but the showing of the rescript to the Ordinary, it must be observed that this act, though not necessary, is at least very becoming, inasmuch as the diocesan Bishop is the proper guardian of law and discipline in his territory. Hence, in

18 C. 14, 6°, I, 3.
19 Cfr. c. 28, X, I, 3.

20 Cfr. cc. 4, 27, 6°, III, 4 de praebendis.

rescripts giving faculties for various blessings the clausula is found, "*cum consensu Ordinarii.*"

CAN. 50

In dubio, rescripta quae ad lites referuntur, vel iura aliis quaesita laedunt, vel adversantur legi in commodum privatorum, vel denique impetrata fuerunt ad beneficii ecclesiastici assecutionem, strictam interpretationem recipiunt; cetera omnia latam.

In case of doubt, rescripts which pertain to disputes, or which trench on the acquired rights of others, or which reverse the law in favor of private parties, or, finally, which were given for the attainment of an ecclesiastical benefice, demand a strict interpretation; all others may be interpreted broadly.

The following canons state the duty of presentation as limited by certain conditions.

CAN. 51

Rescriptum Sedis Apostolicae in quo nullus datur exsecutor, tunc tantum debet Ordinario impetrantis praesentari, cum id in eisdem litteris praecipitur, aut de rebus agitur publicis, aut comprobare conditiones quasdam oportet.

A rescript of the Apostolic See which designates no executor must be presented to the Ordinary of the petitioner only in case the presentation is enjoined in the document itself, or if there is question of public affairs, or if there are conditions that are subject to probation [*i. e.,* ascertaining the truth].

The first condition is evident. The second, which concerns public acts (*de rebus agitur publicis*), seems to refer to such rescripts as contain a favor to be used publicly. Such favors would be, for instance, privileges attached to a sanctuary or benefice, or a distinctive ecclesiastical dress, or permission to collect alms.[21] The last condition evidently has reference to rescripts regarding oratories, matrimonial dispensations, etc.

As to the *time* within which rescripts must be presented, canon 52 states:

CAN. 52

Rescripta, quorum praesentationi nullum est definitum tempus, possunt exsecutori exhiberi quovis tempore, modo absit fraus et dolus.

Rescripts for the presentation of which no definite time is set, may be exhibited to the executor at any time, provided fraud and deceit are excluded.

Note that this canon does not distinguish between rescripts of justice and rescripts of favor,[22] but embraces both kinds, provided only fraud and deceit be avoided; for fraud and deceit deserve no indulgence and are contrary to the spirit of order.

21 Cfr. c. 6, X, I, 3 concerning Cistercians, who may collect tithes without heeding an apostolic rescript, unless mention is made therein of that privilege.

22 Formerly rescripts of justice had to be presented within a year from the date of receipt; the Code makes no distinction between the two species of rescripts in this regard.

THE OFFICE OF EXECUTOR

We said above that it is the rule to choose an " executor " to investigate the matter and persons demanding a rescript. Certain duties, therefore, are incumbent on the executor, who may become the cause of grave mistakes which render a rescript invalid. Therefore the following canons more closely describe the functions of the executor.

CAN. 53

Rescripti exsecutor invalide munere suo fungitur, antequam litteras receperit earumque authenticitatem et integritatem recognoverit, nisi praevia earundem notitia ad eum fuerit auctoritate rescribentis transmissa.

The executor of a rescript acts invalidly if he acts before he has received the letters and determined their authenticity and integrity, unless he has been previously informed of their contents by authority of the grantor.

Hence, as soon as the executor has received the document, he must look at the signature and the seal, to ascertain whence it came; for this is to establish authenticity. Then he may peruse the contents, assuring himself that nothing substantial is wanting and that all the necessary papers are included. After that he will determine the subject-matter or nature of the case. Then he must carefully ponder over the clausulae, which contain certain conditions for the executor as well as the petitioner. Before he has done all this the executor cannot validly proceed to carry out the rescript, unless he

has been informed by telegraph, telephone or other means
as to the contents of the document. This information
must come from the grantor or an official connected with
the grantor. Next he must ascertain from the *clausulae*
whether he is an *exsecutor necessarius* or *voluntarius*.
Thus, *e. g.,* " *si constiterit* " or " *constito tibi,*" " *conscien-
tiam tuam oneramus,*" [28] etc., are indicative of an *exsecutor voluntarius* (or at least *mixtus*), whilst the absence of
such clauses permits one to presume that he is merely an
exsecutor necessarius, i. e., one who simply delivers the
rescript. However, even if he is an *exsecutor necessarius*
and cannot refuse the granting of the favor, circumstances may be such as to cause him to withhold the
execution. Three cases only are enumerated.

CAN. 54

§ 1. Si in rescripto committatur merum exsecutionis
ministerium, exsecutio rescripti denegari non potest,
nisi aut manifeste pateat rescriptum vitio subreptionis
aut obreptionis nullum esse, aut in rescripto appo-
nantur conditiones quas exsecutori constet non esse
impletas, aut qui rescriptum impetravit adeo, iudicio
exsecutoris, videatur indignus ut aliorum offensioni
futura sit gratiae concessio; quod ultimum si accidat,
exsecutor, intermissa exsecutione, statim ea de re cer-
tiorem faciat rescribentem.

§ 2. Quod si in rescripto concessio gratiae exsecutori
committatur, ipsius est pro suo prudenti arbitrio et
conscientia gratiam concedere vel denegare.

---

28 This clausula is not, properly
speaking, conditional, but intended
to render the executor cautious. It
means that the business is committed to the prudence of an honest
man with common sense, who must
follow the dictates of legal justice,
but it also signifies that the executor
cannot subdelegate his office. Cfr.
Barbosa, *Tractatus Varii,* de clausulis, cl. 24, p. 274.

§ 1. If a rescript commissions the executor merely to carry out its terms, he is not allowed to refuse to do so, unless it is evident that the rescript is void in consequence of a *subreptio* or *obreptio,* or the executor is satisfied that the conditions appended to the rescript are not fulfilled, or if the petitioner, in the judgment of the executor, is so unworthy of the favor granted that the grant would prove offensive to others; in the last-mentioned case the executor should not proceed to execute his commission but immediately notify the grantor.

§ 2. If the granting of a favor is committed to the executor, the latter may either grant or deny it, according to his prudent judgment and conscience.

As to the first point: The executor is supposed to know the circumstances of the petitioner, *e. g.,* in matrimonial dispensations, and as a rule it is not difficult for him to judge whether or not the truth has been concealed. *Obreptio* and *subreptio* are mentioned, hence the executor is bound to investigate the existence or absence of the reasons alleged.

As to the second point, it will be noticed that the conditions must be fulfilled at the time of the execution, but nothing is said about the future. Hence all the conditions for a private oratory, for instance, must be previously complied with, whereas, in a rescript for a mixed marriage the future fulfillment of the conditions need not concern the executor.

As to the third point, it may be noted that the position of the executor may become very ticklish because of the vagueness of the term *indignus* (unworthy). If we speak of one being *indignus* in an election, we mean that he lacks the required qualities. Perhaps a more reliable standard is furnished by a comparison with the refusal of administering the sacraments to " *indigne petentibus.*" An " *indignus* " in the sense of our canon therefore is probably a public sinner.[24] The grant may be offensive to the faithful or to others, to whom it might give an occasion to belittle the Church. If that be the case, the executor is bound to postpone the execution and inform the grantor.

If the executor is a *voluntarius, i. e.,* may either grant or refuse the favor according to his good judgment and conscience, all depends upon him and he must bear the consequences of his action. There is one notable consequence attending such a form of commission, *viz.,* that the rescript expires with the death of the executor.[25]

Can. 55

Exsecutor procedere debet ad mandati normam, et nisi conditiones essentiales in litteris appositas impleverit ac substantialem procedendi formam servaverit, irrita est exsecutio.

The executor is obliged to proceed as if he had received a mandate, and unless he shall have fulfilled the essential conditions laid down in the rescript, and followed in substance the required

[24] A notorious Freemason, or a persecutor of the Church and hierarchy, a *concubinarius publicus,* all these would fall under the category of *indigni.*

[25] " Arbitrium expirat morte illius, qui illud habet "; cfr. Barbosa, claus. 11, p. 364.

form of proceeding, the execution is invalid.

A *mandatum*, broadly speaking, is a rescript by which a superior commands or prescribes something. There are two kinds of *mandatum* which may here come into question: the *mandatum apostolicum*, used in the provision or conferring of benefices, and the *mandatum procuratorium*, by which one is made procurator or empowered to act as proxy.[26] The latter is here to be considered, and what is said in general about a mandate of proxy applies to the present case, and therefore the executor must observe the form of the mandate. This he does if he grants neither more nor less than is expressed in the rescript, *e. g.*, if the rescript permits a secularization *ad tempus*, the executor cannot grant it *in perpetuum*. He must furthermore observe the limits of the mandate as to persons, time, and conditions.[27] Finally, in rescripts of justice, the executor must follow the summary procedure explained in Book IV.

CAN. 56

Exsecutio rescriptorum quae forum externum respiciunt, scripto facienda est.

The execution of rescripts which affect the external forum must be made in writing.

CAN. 57

§ 1. Rescriptorum exsecutor potest alium pro suo prudenti arbitrio sibi substituere, nisi substitutio prohibita fuerit, aut substituti persona praefinita.

---

26 Reiffenstuel, I, 3, 21; I, 38, nn. 72 ff.; de procuratoribus.

27 Barbosa, *l. c.*, Axioma 144:

"quia paria sunt, non habere mandatum vel non servare formam mandati."

§ 2. Si tamen fuerit electa industria personae, exsecutori non licet alteri committere, nisi actus praeparatorios.

§ 1. The executor of a rescript may, if he prudently judges fit, appoint another in his place, unless such substitution is forbidden or some other person has been designated.

§ 2. If, however, an executor has been chosen by reason of his personal qualities, he may not delegate his office to another, but only the preliminary acts.

Can. 58

Rescripta quaelibet exsecutioni mandari possunt etiam ab exsecutoris successore in dignitate vel officio, nisi fuerit electa industria personae.

A rescript may be executed by the successor in dignity or office of the original executor, unless the latter had been appointed on account of his personal qualities.

Since the code mentions no special reason for not attending personally to the affair, it is left to the executor to delegate another. Thus a Bishop may give general permission to his Vicar-general or Chancellor to attend to such matters unless such action is either expressly or implicitly forbidden; for it may be that a law does not allow the Ordinary to give such a general permission, which cases will be noted in the course of this commentary. Besides, if the executor is chosen for his *personal qualities, e. g.,* his knowledge or acquaintance with the case and the persons involved, or for peculiar merit, substitution is not permissible. The same holds good concerning the successor in dignity or office. *Dignity* here means jurisdiction and precedence, not merely dignitaries, for such do not succeed one other. Whether the term *office* is to be taken in the general sense of an ecclesiastical office, or in the stricter sense of *officium*, which implies neither jurisdiction nor precedence but only administration, is not stated, but the text seems to indicate the latter. Hence, *e. g.*, the custodian of a cathedral church or the secretary or chancellor of a Bishop, are officials to the practical intent of this canon.[28]

CAN. 59

§ 1. Exsecutori fas est, si quoquo modo in rescriptorum exsecutione erraverit, iterum eadem exsecutioni mandare.

§ 2. Quod attinet ad taxas pro rescriptorum exsecutione, servetur praescriptum can. 1507, § 1.

§ 1. If an executor has made a mistake of any kind in the execution of a rescript, he has the right to repeat the execution.

§ 2. As regards the fees for the execution of a rescript, canon 1507, § 1 must be observed.

The fees for the execution of rescripts are governed by well-defined rules for each ecclesiastical province, which rules are prescribed by the Holy See, to whom also is reserved the approbation of taxation laws to be followed in a province (can. 1507).

---

28 Cfr. Barbosa, *Tractatus Varii*, Appellatio 126, p. 269; the custos of a cathedral or collegiate chapter is looked upon as a *personatus* (cf. Book II, on cathedral chapters).

RECALL AND CESSATION OF RESCRIPTS

The effect of a rescript — except it be a mere faculty — generally lasts forever or at least as long as the reason for which the petition was made. But it may be revoked. Hence

CAN. 60

§ 1. Rescriptum, per peculiarem Superioris actum revocatum, perdurat usque dum revocatio ei, qui illud obtinuit, significetur.

§ 2. Per legem contrariam nulla rescripta revocantur, nisi aliud in ipsa lege caveatur, aut lex lata sit a Superiore ipsius rescribentis.

§ 1. If a rescript is revoked by a special act of a superior, it does not lose its validity until the revocation has been duly intimated to the petitioner.

§ 2. No rescript is recalled by a contrary law, unless the law expressly so provides, or unless it is given by the superior of the one who granted the rescript.

CAN. 61

Per Apostolicae Sedis aut dioecesis vacationem nullum eiusdem Sedis Apostolicae aut Ordinarii rescriptum perimitur, nisi aliud ex additis clausulis appareat, aut rescriptum contineat potestatem alicui factam concedendi gratiam peculiaribus personis in eodem expressis, et res adhuc integra sit.

A rescript does not lose its force by reason of the vacancy of the Holy See or of a diocese, unless

the contrary appears from the respective
clausulae, or unless the rescript conveys the power
of granting a favor to particular persons expressly named therein, and the matter has not yet
been made the subject of litigation.

A rescript might be repealed by the issuing of another
rescript, but unless the second rescript mentions the former as abolished, the former rescript remains in force.
Here the act of repeal is not express and explicit and
must be formally intimated to the petitioner or owner
of the rescript. However, a sort of tacit recall is admitted, *viz.,* by a *contrary law,* which must expressly mention the rescripts recalled or must have been issued by
the superior of the one who issued the rescript. This
latter clause evidently refers to the Pope in regard to a
Bishop who may have granted a rescript, and means that
the Sovereign Pontiff may cancel a rescript issued by an
Ordinary. But here the rules of interpreting laws must
be applied. The canon properly speaks of *expiring* rescripts. It was formerly held that rescripts of justice
expired with the death or resignation of the grantor, *re
adhuc integra.* But canon 61 makes no such distinction,
and hence a rescript does not become extinct by the death
of the pontiff or bishop who gave it. An exception is
made when there is a clause signifying the intention of
the grantor to concede the favor granted only during his
life-time or for a certain limited period. *Clausulae* of
that kind would apparently be the following: "*usque ad
beneplacitum nostrum,*" "*usque ad beneplacitum Sedis
Apostolicae,*" "*donec revocavero.*" The first clausula
would extinguish a rescript [29] at the death of the grantor,

29 Cf. c. 5, 6°, I, 3; cf. can. 73; the opinion of Laurentius, *Inst.*

but the second ("*usque ad benep. S. Ap.*") would not, because the Apostolic See does not die;[30] nor does the last ("*donec revocavero*"), according to weighty authors, extinguish the rescript, because, they say, a positive act is required for the repeal of a rescript,[31] an opinion which seems to be supported by canon 60, § 1.

The other condition under which a rescript elapses at the death of the grantor consists in the direct faculty given to the executor to grant a favor to specially named persons. For in that case the executor acts as procurator, — at least this seems to be the underlying principle,— who has received a special mandate, which naturally ceases with the death of the *mandans*, unless the business has taken a juridical turn (*res adhuc integra*) and the juridical stage has been reached, if citations or summons have been legally issued or the parties have spontaneously appeared before the judge, or in this case, before the executor.[32]

The last canon of this title, which certainly has been dealt with liberally in our Code, says that if a rescript contains a privilege or dispensation, the rules for privileges and dispensations laid down in the following canons must be observed.

CAN. 62

Si rescriptum contineat non simplicem gratiam, sed privilegium vel dispensationem, serventur insuper praescripta canonum qui sequuntur.

If a rescript contains, not a simple favor, but a

Iuris Eccl., n. 296, is destitute of foundation.

30 Cf. c. 5, 6°, I, 3.

31 Cf. Barbosa, *l. c.*, claus. 43, p. 402; Reiffenstuel, I, 3, n. 263.

32 Cf. can. 1725, which settles the controversy about the moment when a matter ceases to be *integra*.

privilege or dispensation, then besides [the rules laid down in the preceding canons] the regulations established in the following canons must be observed.

TITLE V

ON PRIVILEGES

A special class of laws is that dealing with privileges. A privilege (*privilegium, lex privata*) may be defined as " a more or less permanent concession made by the legislator against (or beyond) the law." [1]

A privilege is a *law,* and hence falls under the power of the legislator only in so far as he can establish laws. If a privilege contains a concession which the law prohibits, it is a privilege *against the law.* If a privilege grants a right beyond what the law has already granted, it is said to go *beyond the law (praeter jus),* as *e. g.,* the privilege of absolving from reserved cases. Properly speaking only a *privilege against the law* is truly a privilege,[2] though faculties are justly enumerated among the *privileges beyond the law* (can. 66, § 1).

HISTORICAL NOTE

It is evident that the theory of privileges must have developed apace with the practice of the Roman See. Though privileges were granted and revoked by the popes before the great collections of ecclesiastic law were made, the doctrinal exposition of privileges began with Gratian.[8] In a famous dictum the Magister solves the objection raised by the necessity of strictly observing the canons of councils and the decrees of popes as follows: The

---

1 Cf. tit. 33, bk. V, Decretal., and the commentators thereon, for instance, Engel, Reiffenstuel, and Suarez, *De Legibus.*

2 Reiffenstuel, *l. c.,* n. 8.
8 Cf. dictum ad c. 16, C. 25, q. 1; c. 30, C. 11, q. 1; c. 4, C. 24, q. 1.

Roman Church has the authority to establish laws, but she is not bound by them, because she is the head and support (*caput et cardo*) of all the churches, and all laws have attached to them the implicit clause, "*salvo jure sanctae Romanae Ecclesiae.*" Hence if privileges are granted which apparently are against the common law, they do not clash with the right of the Church, because all privileges are reserved to her. From this point of view it followed, of course, that no privilege would be granted except for the honor and utility of the Church, and that privileges were revocable. Gratian's teaching was an innovation only in so far as this principle had not been laid down in any law-book before him. But in substance it simply embodied the practice which the Roman Court had followed for about a century. As the papal power developed under the "protection of St. Peter," the theory of privileges assumed a more detailed and definite form. This was the case especially in the eleventh and twelfth centuries.[4] We must add that in course of time clerical privileges and exemptions to a great extent lost their original character of privileges and became, as it were, part and parcel of the common law.

DIVISION OF PRIVILEGES

Manifold is the division of privileges. It will suffice for our purpose to note the following:

a) A *personal* privilege is one granted to a person for a reason inherent exclusively in that person, *e. g.*, the wearing of the cappa magna or purple skullcap, if given not to the office but to the person. A *real* privilege is one attached to a thing, place, office, or dignity; *e. g.*, the *privilegium altaris* or a privilege given to a sanctuary.

[4] Cf. Saegmueller in the *Tüb. Quartalschrift*, 1907, p. 93 ff.

A *mixed* privilege is one granted to a corporation or society or confraternity as such.

b) A *favorable* privilege is one containing a mere favor, without prejudice to a third person. An *odious* privilege is one involving prejudice or detriment to another, *e. g.*, freedom from taxation or tithes.

c) Privileges are granted in various *forms*, either in writing or by word of mouth, either *motu proprio* or by petition, either absolutely (*per se*) or *ad instar*. A privilege granted in *writing* is always safer. A written document is required where injury to another is involved, unless an orally granted privilege can be proved by witnesses. Otherwise an *oral* privilege may be used personally as long as no legitimate authority or injured third party demands proof (can. 79).

d) A privilege given *absolutely* or *per se* is one granted without respect or reference to pre-existing privileges. A privilege *ad instar* refers directly to a pre-existing pattern. Thus, *e. g.*, most of the privileges granted to religious and confraternities are *ad instar*.

ACQUISITION OF PRIVILEGES

A privilege being a law in favor of private persons, proceeds from the same power as the law. Hence the Sovereign Pontiff can grant privileges against the common ecclesiastical law, but not against the natural or divine law. It matters little, *per se,* whether he concedes these privileges in writing or orally (*vivae vocis oraculo*), directly, *i. e.*, absolutely, or indirectly, *i. e., ad instar*, for he has the power to choose the mode of granting privileges. Hence the first canon of this title declares that privileges may be obtained both by direct concession and communication and through legitimate custom or prescription, and that centennial or immemorial possession creates a presumption in favor of a privilege.

CAN. 63

§ 1. Privilegia acquiri possunt non solum per directam concessionem competentis auctoritatis et per communicationem, sed etiam per legitimam consuetudinem aut praescriptionem.

§ 2. Possessio centenaria vel immemorabilis inducit praesumptionem concessi privilegii.

§ 1. Privileges can be acquired not only by direct concession on the part of legitimate authority and by communication, but likewise by legitimate custom or prescription.

§ 2. Centenary or immemorial possession of a privilege is a presumption in favor of its genuineness.

There is, then, a threefold way of acquiring ecclesiastical privileges: by direct concession on the part of a competent authority (pope or bishop), by communication, and by prescription.

The first is evident and needs no explanation.

Communication means partaking of a privilege either by extension or by aggregation (*per connectionem*). Thus if a confraternity is aggregated to an archconfraternity, it shares the privileges of the latter. A privilege may be acquired also by *explicit application*, the privileges granted to some being expressly conceded to others in the same manner, measure and form, yet with the effect that the latter grantees enjoy these privileges absolutely and independently of the former. This is called *communicatio plena et absoluta,* or *aeque principalis,* whilst the former is *communicatio imperfecta et relativa* or *accessoria.* A complete and absolute communication of privileges formerly took place between all mendicant orders. Excepted from communication are the so-called " exorbitant " privileges and such as are styled " incommunicable." [5]

The third method of acquiring a privilege is by *custom* or *prescription.* This has been the general teaching of canonists, based on a famous decretal of Innocent III. In this decretal the words *" contraria consuetudo "* occur,[6] and, since all canonists insisted on prescription, they simply said: *" privilegium potest acquiri praescriptione seu consuetudine legitime praescripta."* [7] This *opinio communis* receives, as it were, official sanction in the present canon.

The length of time required for prescription must be measured according to canons 27 f., quoted above; it is, besides, determined more closely by § 2 of can. 63.

Possession here means, not only actual occupation but the right of possessing a thing.[8] Such possession lasting for a century or time immemorial creates a *presumption* that the privilege is real and authentic. This presumption, not being further described, is to be taken as a simple *praesumptio juris,* which must cede to truth if conclusively disproved. Thus, *e. g.,* if it be proved that regulars who have held a parish for forty or more years, never obtained a privilege to that effect, the Bishop can claim the parish for the secular clergy.

[5] Only if a Bull contains the words, " etiam incommunicabilia," are these privileges included; see. *e. g.,* the Const. of Urban VIII, " Plantata," of July 12, 1633, in the *Bullarium Cong. Angl. O.S.B.,* 1912, pp. 5 ff.

[6] C. 13, Novit., X, II, 1 de judiciis.

[7] Reiffenstuel, V, 33, n. 39.

[8] " Detentio rei corporis et animi et juris adminiculo."

The legislator now turns to the second mode of acquiring a privilege, which is more subject to abuse.

CAN. 64

Per communicationem privilegiorum, etiam in forma aeque principali, ea tantum privilegia impertita censentur, quae directe, perpetuo et sine speciali relatione ad certum locum aut rem aut personam concessa fuerant primo privilegiario, habita etiam ratione capacitatis subiecti, cui fit communicatio.

In the communication of privileges, even that called *aeque principalis,* only those privileges are included which were imparted to the original grantee directly, forever, and without special relation to a certain place, thing or person, and with due consideration of the capability of the receiver.

Evidently the Code wishes to clear up the nature of *communicatio,* especially as espoused by religious orders; yet, in the main, it adopts the ancient solid doctrine. Privileges which were *not directly* granted cannot be communicated. This provision is perhaps new, but it is wholesome, for otherwise privileges might be claimed over which the legislator has no control, and unduly multiplied. Religious orders under this canon cannot by communication claim a privilege which was already granted to another order by communication. However, this law is not retroactive, and hence the orders may retain what they possess, except where the Code rules differently.

A privilege, to be communicable, must have been

granted *forever.* Therefore spiritual favors granted *ad quinquennium, e. g.,* are not communicable.[9]

Lastly, privileges granted to *particular* persons, places, or things cannot be transferred to others. For instance, the privilege of wearing a purple skullcap, given on account of personal merit and distinction, the privilege given to a special sanctuary or to a particular altar or sacred object, are incommunicable.

Note, too, that the persons or subjects to whom a communication of privilege is made, are capable thereof only in so far as their condition and position render them apt. Thus nuns (*moniales*) are not capable of enjoying all the privileges granted to monks or regulars, *e. g.,* that of preaching, absolving, etc., although they may be capable of others.

The following canon determines the *extent* of a *communicatio accessoria* (*ad instar*):

CAN. 65

Cum privilegia acquiruntur per communicationem in forma accessoria, augentur, imminuuntur vel amittuntur ipso facto, si forte augeantur, imminuantur vel cessent in principali privilegiario; secus si acquirantur per communicationem in forma aeque principali.

Privileges acquired by communication in *forma accessoria,* are increased, diminished or lost to the second grantee in proportion to their increase, decrease, or loss in the original grantee; which rule is not, however, to be applied to the *communicatio absoluta* or *aeque principalis.*

[9] Cf. Antonius de Spiritu S., Ord. Carm., *Directorium Regular.,* tract. I, disp. 1, sectio 3, n. 42.

Hence, if an archconfraternity loses a part or all of its indulgences, they are also lost to the aggregated confraternities. This rule does not hold good in the communication of religious orders, wherefore, if one religious community were suppressed, another, which had received a privilege from it by communication, might continue to enjoy the same.

FACULTIES

A special canon treats of *faculties,* which term here means certain rights denied by common law but granted by special privilege. It follows from the nature of a faculty that it can be given only by one who can modify the common law. This one is primarily the Pope, though bishops also may grant faculties concerning matters subject to their legislation.[10] Since the sixteenth century special faculties were granted chiefly to the German bishops, and classified in certain formularies, *pro foro externo* and *pro foro interno, quinquennales* and *triennales,* and for a determined number of cases.[11] Their object is as wide as ecclesiastical discipline itself, and comprises especially dispensations, absolutions, and licenses for performing acts otherwise prohibited by law, *e. g.,* reading forbidden books.

The Code says with regard to these faculties:

CAN. 66

§ 1. Facultates habituales quae conceduntur vel in

10 For instance, hearing confessions, preaching, etc.

11 Cf. Putzer, *Comment. in Facult. apost.,* 1897, ed. 4.—For the formularies containing the faculties granted to the bishops of the U. S. see Sabetti-Barrett, *Theol. Mo-*

ralis, 1917. p. 1081 ff. These faculties, His Excellency the Apostolic Delegate, Most Rev. J. Bonzano, had the kindness to inform the author, are *extraordinary,* and therefore liable to modification or repeal.

perpetuum vel ad praefinitum tempus aut certum numerum casuum, accensentur privilegiis praeter ius.

§ 2. Nisi in earum concessione electa fuerit industria personae aut aliud expresse cautum sit, facultates habituales, Episcopo aliisve de quibus in can. 198, § 1 ab Apostolica Sede concessae, non evanescunt, resoluto iure Ordinarii cui concessae sunt, etiamsi ipse eas exsequi coeperit, sed transeunt ad Ordinarios qui ipsi in regimine succedunt; item concessae Episcopo competunt quoque Vicario Generali.

§ 3. Concessa facultas secumfert alias quoque potestates quae ad illius usum sunt necessariae; quare in facultate dispensandi includitur etiam potestas absolvendi a poenis ecclesiasticis, si quae forte obstent, sed ad effectum dumtaxat dispensationis consequendae.

§ 1. Habitual faculties, granted for ever, or for a limited time, or for a definite number of cases, are reckoned among privileges beyond the law.

§ 2. Unless they were conceded for personal reasons, or unless the law provides otherwise, habitual faculties do not expire with the authority of the Ordinary (or others; see can. 198, § 1) to whom they have been granted by the Apostolic See, even though he may have begun to execute them, but pass over to those who succeed him in office; faculties granted to the Bishop are intended also for the Vicar General.

§ 3. A faculty implies all the powers necessary for its exercise; hence the faculty of dispensing includes the faculty of absolving from censures, if necessary, but only for the purpose of receiving the dispensation.

As to § 1 note: Habitual faculties are those which are commonly granted to bishops either for a certain time or for a limited number of cases, and are, as it were, concomitants of the episcopal office. As they are numbered among *privileges,* the rules of interpreting privileges must be applied to them, *ceteris paribus.*

As to § 2: These habitual faculties do not expire with the cessation of the Ordinary's term of office, but continue in his successors, and the faculties granted to the Bishop are also given to the Vicar General, unless the Bishop (or others to whom the faculties were given) was selected for this honor on account of personal qualities. The name " Ordinary " is applied to diocesan bishops, each for his territory, to Abbots *Nullius,* and to the Vicars-general of both, to Apostolic Vicars and Prefects, and to the Superiors of exempt religious.[12] The successor of the Ordinary to whom a faculty was granted, may complete the execution thereof which the predecessor had begun, *e. g.,* by calling witnesses, issuing summonses, etc.

As to § 3: A faculty, if given, grants the use of all the means necessary for its application, and hence the faculty of dispensing includes the power of absolving from censures, when necessary; but only for the purpose of rendering the subject capable of receiving the dispensation. Therefore, *e. g.,* an excommunication or suspension or personal interdict is, *de facto,* suspended only here and now, whilst conditions added to the censures for the case of real absolution remain.

12 Cfr. can. 198 and the declaration of the Holy Office of Feb. 20, 1888; when the term *" loci "* or *" locorum "* is added, the superiors of exempt orders are not included.

Can. 67

Privilegium ex ipsius tenore aestimandum est, nec licet illud extendere aut restringere.

A privilege must be interpreted according to its wording or purport, and must be neither extended nor restricted.

Can. 68

In dubio privilegia interpretanda sunt ad normam can. 50; sed ea semper adhibenda interpretatio, ut privilegio aucti aliquam ex indulgentia concedentis videantur gratiam consecuti.

In case of doubt privileges must be interpreted in accordance with can. 50, but in such a way that those who have received the privilege always retain some favor from the good will of the grantor.

The interpretation of privileges follows the general rules of interpretation, as stated above, and especially that of rescripts. The principal rule is that the wording or purport (*tenor*) of the text must be duly consulted. Neither an extensive nor a restrictive interpretation of privileges is admissible. Where a doubt exists, the rule given in can. 50 must be applied, but in such a way that some privilege or favor remains.

Can. 69

Nemo cogitur uti privilegio in sui dumtaxat favorem concesso, nisi alio ex capite exsurgat obligatio.

No one is obliged to make use of a privilege

granted to him solely for his own benefit, unless an obligation to that effect should arise from some other source.

CAN. 70

Privilegium, nisi aliud constet, censendum est perpetuum.

A privilege is perpetual, unless the contrary is evident.

A doubt may arise as to whether a privilege is purely personal, or real, or mixed. Such doubts can be solved by examining the subject-matter and the wording of the privilege. The purpose or scope of a privilege is, as a rule, obvious. If it is not clear whether the successor of a personally privileged Ordinary, *e. g.*, the successor of an abbot, has the use of a certain privilege, the address of the document should be examined. If the name of the grantee appears first, and his dignity second, the privilege must be regarded as merely personal. Where the dignity is mentioned first, the privilege may be taken as real and is consequently transferable to the successor in the same dignity or office, unless the wording of the text excludes this interpretation.[18]

The Code adds, *" nisi alio ex capite exsurgat obligatio,"* thereby no doubt referring to the so-called personal privileges of the clergy which cannot be renounced by the individual. It may also be that the fulfillment of a precept would urge, for instance, hearing Mass in a private oratory,[14] or absolving or dispensing, etc. Unless the contrary is clearly expressed, a privilege lasts for ever.

---

18 Cfr. Engel, V, 33, n. 4.
14 Laurentius, *Inst. Iuris Eccl.*, 1903, p. 247.

Although its nature would seem to spell perpetuity, a privilege may be lost, either by law, or lapse, or renunciation, or by one's own fault.

CAN. 71

Per legem generalem revocantur privilegia in hoc Codice contenta; ad cetera quod attinet, servetur praescriptum can. 60.

A general law repeals the privileges contained in this Code; otherwise can. 60 concerning the recall of rescripts must be applied.

Formerly a certain class of privileges was called "*clausa in corpore juris*" and sometimes "*privilegia in corpore juris clauso*," which signified those privileges contained in the Corpus Juris.[15] In like manner the privileges contained in the New Code, *e. g.*, clerical, religious, and real, form a special class, and as such may be abolished by a general law issued by the supreme lawgiver.

CAN. 72

§ 1. Privilegia cessant per renuntiationem a competente Superiore acceptatam.

§ 2. Privilegio in sui tantum favorem constituto quaevis persona privata renuntiare potest.

§ 3. Concesso alicui communitati, dignitati, locove renuntiare privatis personis non licet.

§ 4. Nec ipsi communitati seu coetui integrum est renuntiare privilegio sibi dato per modum legis, vel si

15 The authors, however, did not agree as to what constituted the " Corpus Juris," some admitting only the three authentic collections, others including the Decretum and the Extravagantes.

renuntiatio cedat in ecclesiae aliorumve praeiudicium.

§ 1. Privileges cease by renunciation if the renunciation is accepted by the competent superior.

§ 2. A merely personal privilege may be given up by any private person.

§ 3. A privilege granted to a community, dignity, or place cannot be renounced by private persons.

§ 4. Nor is the community or congregation (society) itself free to renounce a privilege granted by way of law, or if its renunciation should cause a prejudice to the Church or to others.

For a commentary on this point see p. 167, *infra.*

Can. 73

Resoluto iure concedentis, privilegia non exstinguuntur, nisi data fuerint cum clausula: *ad beneplacitum nostrum*, vel alia aequipollenti.

Privileges are not extinguished even if the grantor goes out of office, unless they contain the clause: *ad beneplacitum nostrum,* or some other clause of like import.

A clause of like import would be, *e. g.,* " *durante pontificatu.*"

Can. 74

Privilegium personale personam sequitur et cum ipsa exstinguitur.

A personal privilege follows the person to whom it has been granted and expires with that person.

Here a note may be allowed as to the first clause. While it is true that the personal privilege cleaves, as the canonists say, to the bones of the person, the use of such a privilege may be limited or perhaps subject to the consent of another. Thus, *e. g.*, the wearing of the Cappa Magna is granted to some abbots not in virtue of their office, but to the person, and hence is restricted to their own churches.

CAN. 75

Privilegia realia cessant per absolutum rei vel loci interitum; privilegia vero localia, si locus intra quinquaginta annos restituatur, reviviscunt.

Real privileges cease upon the complete destruction of the thing or place, whilst local privileges revive if the place is restored within fifty years.

This enactment is of great importance for churches and monasteries, which, though the new proprietors or occupants have no relation whatever with the former, can enjoy their privileges without an act of renewal, if only a record be kept of the time of ruin and restoration. Of course it is understood that the restored places serve the same purpose as before,— the purpose for which, or in view of which, the privilege was given.

Renunciation of a privilege (as dealt with in canon 72, *supra*) is the voluntary giving up of a privilege acquired.[16] This is permissible because, as a rule, everyone is at liberty to relinquish his own rights.[17] However, to be effective, renunciation must be accepted by competent authority. Hence

§ 1 says that privileges cease by renunciation if the latter is accepted by the competent authority, which is none other than the grantor or his legitimate successors.

According to § 2, a merely personal privilege may be surrendered by any private person. The reason is because such privileges are supposed to affect the holder exclusively.

§ 3 declares that a privilege granted to a community, dignity or place cannot be renounced by private persons. It follows that the superior of a community, or a religious, or a clergyman cannot renounce such a privilege, *e. g.*, of exemption or the *privilegium canonis* and *fori.*[18]

§ 4 provides that not even a community or congregation is free to renounce a privilege if it has been granted by way of law, or if its renunciation would cause a prejudice to the Church or to others. A privilege granted by way of law is one contained in the Code, *e. g.*, clerical exemption, immunity. Such a privilege cannot be renounced, even if the community by common consent, or an assembly by general assent or a majority of votes, were ready to give it up. It is also forbidden to renounce a privilege, even though not contained in the Code, if

16 " Resoluto juris concedentis " (rescribentis, ferentis legem) is an expression often occurring in the Code, and is of general purport, including every kind of cessation of office by death, resignation, transfer, exchange, suspension, or deposition.

17 C. 6, X, V, 33.

18 Cfr. c. 12, X, II, 2; c. 36, X, V, 39; c. 5, X, I, 43: "Cum etsi sponte volueris, de jure tamen nequiveris, sine licentia Rom. Pontificis renunciare privilegiis vel indulgentiis libertatis, quae monasterium illud indicant ad jus et proprietatem Rom. Ecclesiae pertinere."

giving it up would result in detriment to the Church or others, *e. g.*, the faculty of binating or absolving from reserved cases. On the other hand, a community or chapter *may* give up such privileges as have become more or less useless or of little importance.[19] A sort of tacit renunciation seems to be what canon 76 calls *non-usus* or contrary usage.

Can. 76

Per non usum vel per usum contrarium privilegia aliis haud onerosa non cessant; quae vero in aliorum gravamen cedunt, amittuntur, si accedat legitima praescriptio vel tacita renuntiatio.

By non-use or contrary use a privilege which is not injurious to others does not cease; but a privilege that is burdensome to others loses its force by legitimate prescription or tacit renunciation.

It may be useful to recall the distinction between an onerous and a non-onerous privilege. The former causes a burden or damage to others, *e. g.*, collecting tithes or alms, whilst the privilege of eating flesh-meat on certain days cannot be called injurious to others (except perhaps to the cook or the treasury).

There is also a difference between *prescription* and *tacit renunciation*. Prescription means a certain space of time, say forty years, during which the privilege has not been made use of, although there was occasion for using it. *Tacit renunciation* means that one has knowingly and willingly performed an act contrary to the privi-

19 Cfr. c. 8, X, I, 2 de const.

lege, either negatively by not using the privilege when one should have used it, or positively, by doing the contrary to that which the privilege entitled one to.[20] The canon says that only onerous privileges, namely, such as follow the *jus patronatus* or right of presentation, cease by non-use or contrary use.[21]

CAN. 77

Cessat quoque privilegium, si temporis progressu rerum adiuncta sic, iudicio Superioris, immutentur ut noxium evaserit, aut eius usus illicitus fiat; item elapso tempore vel expleto numero casuum pro quibus privilegium fuit concessum, firmo praescripto can. 207, § 2.

A privilege also ceases if in course of time conditions change to such a degree that, in the judgment of the superior, the privilege becomes harmful or its use illicit; or if the time for which the privilege has been granted expires, or the number of cases for which it was given is full; without detriment, however, to canon 207, § 2.

This canon states what is self-evident under regula juris 61 in 6°: "quod ob gratiam alicuius conceditur, non est in eius dispendium retorquendum." In can. 207, § 2, the *forum internum* is excepted from the rule here laid down.

CAN. 78

Qui abutitur potestate sibi ex privilegio permissa,

---

20 Cf. Reiffenstuel, V, 33, nn. 201 ff.

21 Cf. c. 6, X, V, 33: "De privilegio tamen indulto tanto tem-pore vobis detrahere voluistis." The length of time is not expressed, but forty years may safely be assumed.

privilegio ipso privari meretur; et Ordinarius Sanctam Sedem monere ne omittat, si quis privilegio ab eadem concesso graviter abutatur.

Whoever abuses the power granted to him by a privilege, deserves to be deprived of the privilege itself; and the Ordinary shall not fail to notify the Apostolic See if anyone grievously abuses a privilege granted to him by the same.

The wording of this canon leaves no doubt that abuse does not, *eo ipso,* annul a privilege, but only after a sentence issued by the Apostolic See.[22] By the name of " Ordinary " is meant not only the diocesan Ordinary and his Vicar General, but the superior of exempt religious. On the other hand, it is also true that certain crimes are stated and singled out in the law itself as attended by the loss of certain privileges, *e. g.,* if one commits a crime in a church, presuming on immunity, or fails to wear the clerical dress, of which more *loco suo.*

The last canon on privileges treats of privileges granted *vivae vocis oraculo, i. e.,* by word of mouth.

CAN. 79

Quamvis privilegia, oretenus a Sancta Sede obtenta, ipsi petenti in foro conscientiae suffragentur, nemo tamen potest cuiusvis privilegii usum adversus quemquam in foro externo vindicare, nisi privilegium ipsum sibi concessum esse legitime evincat.

Although privileges orally granted by the Holy See, may be used by the grantee in the internal

---

22 Cf. c. 7, Dist. 74 (Greg. M.); c. 24, X, V, 33; the abuse may touch upon time or place or persons exceeding the limits thereof.

court of conscience, no one should claim their use against another *in foro externo,* unless he can prove that the privilege was legitimately obtained.

For example, I know of a religious who received from Pius X, of happy memory, the privilege of reciting the Breviary, when traveling, according to the rubrics used at S. Anselmo. This privilege was given orally, and consequently touches the conscience rather than the *forum externum.* A privilege for the *forum externum* (*e. g.,* one granted to an order against the jurisdiction of the Ordinary) requires proof. Hither belong the Constitution " Romanus Pontifex," of Gregory XV, of July 2, 1622, and that of Urban VIII, " Alias," of December 20, 1631, which abrogated all *vivae vocis oracula* both *in foro interno* and *externo,* except those obtained by the petitions of sovereigns and cardinals. The new Code admits the existence and use of orally given privileges, as long as conscience alone is concerned; but in justiciable cases such a privilege cannot be alleged, unless proven by witnesses. What witnesses are required? The Code does not specify, but we believe that the testimony of the cardinal-protector of a religious order, or any other cardinal, would be sufficient proof of the privilege having been granted by the Holy See.[23] (Can. 239, § 1, 17.)

In order to complete the subject of privileges, we may be permitted to add a few words on a topic which the Code does not explicitly treat, namely, the *confirmation* or *ratification* of privileges. A privilege may be ratified *in forma communi* or *in forma specifica. Confirmatio in*

23 Cfr. Reiffenstuel, V, 33, nn. 149 ff.

forma communi leaves the value and valor of a privilege
in statu quo, without determining whether the privilege
is valid or invalid, and hence adds no juridical force
either to the first or second grant. *Confirmatio in forma
specifica* is given after mature consideration of the privilege in case, and is executed either by verbal insertion of
the former privilege or by using the clausulae: "*ac si
de verbo ad verbum inserta fuissent,*" or "*ex certa
scientia.*" In this latter case the confirmation gives juridical value to the privilege and is tantamount to a new
valid concession; and the new grantee enjoys the privilege, even if the former should lose it.

Note, also, that privileges are sometimes granted especially by way of communication, or ratified with the
clausula "*dummodo*" or "*quatenus sunt in usu.*" This
means that the grantor does not wish to ratify or grant
anew by corroboration a privilege which has been lost by
non-use or contrary usage, or for another reason.

TITLE VI

ON DISPENSATIONS

It is natural that a society spread over the whole globe and comprising members of the most diverse types living in different climes and under various conditions cannot apply the law with equal rigor at all times and in all circumstances. Even in the first four centuries of her existence the Church was compelled to mitigate the strictness of her penitential discipline. This is briefly and appropriately expressed by Abbo of Fleury (died 1004): " We must take into consideration the situation of countries, the character of the times, the frailty of men, and other reasons which of necessity change the laws of different provinces. The same is true concerning papal decress, which are of such authority that many judges expect the verdict of the Roman Pontiff. In these things, therefore, utility and equity (*utilitas et honestas*) must prevail, but not the enticing enjoyment of desires." [1] The same idea recurs in the prologue to the *Decretum* of Yvo of Chartres (died 1115). He, too, reduces the reasons for granting dispensations to two — utility and necessity, and compares the Church to a crew who throw merchandise over board in order to save the ship. [2] Gratian did not go further, for all his texts are taken from Yvo. [3]

[1] *Collectio Canonum,* c. VIII (Migne, 139, 483), which is untouched by Pseudo-Isidorian influences.

[2] *Proleg. in Decretum* (Migne, 161, 47 ff.).

[3] Cfr. c. 56, Dist. 50; c. 41, C. 1, q. 1; c. 16, C. 1, q. 7.

That with the outward growth of the papacy the power of papal dispensation also increased, goes without saying. Hence it cannot surprise us that Innocent III (1196–1216) said that "the fullness of power confers the right of dispensation."[4] Some bishops and provincial synods also exercised the right of dispensation, although in a limited way. Before Gratian's time, this power touched an accomplished fact rather than something to be done in future, although even this latter species of dispensation (*super faciendum*) was not entirely unknown. Dispensation came to comprise cases of simony, celibacy (especially the *filii presbyterorum*), irregularities, vows, and above all matrimonial cases.[5] The Council of Trent enacted into law what Abbo and Yvo had taught,— that a dispensation should be granted only for urgent and just reasons, for the greater utility of the faithful, and after previous deliberation and cognizance of the case.[6] We shall now see what the new Code has to say on the subject.

Can. 80

Dispensatio, seu legis in casu speciali relaxatio, concedi potest a conditore legis, ab eius successore vel Superiore, nec non ab illo cui iidem facultatem dispensandi concesserint.

A dispensation, *i. e.*, a relaxation of the law in a particular case, may be granted by the lawgiver, his successor or superior, and by those to whom the faculty of dispensing has been delegated.

There is a distinction between *epikeia*, so-called, or

---

[4] Cf. c. 4, X, III, 8.
[5] Cf. Stiegler, *Dispensation, Dispensationswesen und Dispensations-* *recht im Kirchenrecht,* 1901, Vol. I (only one).
[6] Trid., Sess. 25, c. 18 de ref.

benign interpretation, which is related to equity, and a dispensation; for the latter is an act of jurisdiction flowing from the legislative arid judiciary power, whilst the former is nothing more than either an interpretation or an excuse based on private judgment. Hence a dispensation presupposes legislative power, nay is, so to speak, coextensive with it. Therefore the *Pope* can dispense in all matters subject to his legislation, that is to say, in ecclesiastical, but not in divine laws.[7] The same power is vested in his *successor*, because he is his equal, and "*par in parem non habet imperium.*" But the Pope can also dispense from episcopal laws, for he is superior to the bishops. On the other hand a *bishop* may dispense from papal laws if he has received the necessary faculties from the Apostolic See. The same right belongs to *superiors* of exempt religious orders.

The Pope is not bound by the existence or validity of reasons, but can dispense validly without reason, although it is not to be presumed that he would proceed thus, since a dispensation is a sore on the law and should not be used for destruction. This is not the case with those inferior to the Pope, hence canon 81 establishes the power of those *inferior* to the *Roman Pontiff*.

CAN. 81

A generalibus Ecclesiae legibus Ordinarii infra Romanum Pontificem dispensare nequeunt, ne in casu quidem peculiari, nisi haec potestas eisdem fuerit explicite vel implicite concessa, aut nisi difficilis sit recursus ad Sanctam Sedem et simul in mora sit pericu-

---

[7] A difficulty might arise from vows and the *matrimonium ratum;* but in such laws, the obliging force of which depends on the free will of man, the Pontiff can, in virtue of his vicarious power, render the obligation ineffective. (Cfr. Wernz, *l. c.*, I, n. 122.)

lum gravis damni, et de dispensatione agatur quae a Sede Apostolica concedi solet.

Ordinaries inferior to the Pope cannot dispense from the general laws of the Church, not even in a particular case, unless they have received that power either explicitly or implicitly, or in cases in which recourse to the Holy See is difficult and there is at the same time grave danger in delay, and the dispensation requested is one which the Holy See is wont to grant.

Two sources for dispensing, therefore, are open to the Ordinaries, either a communicated power or the nature of the case requiring dispensation. *Explicit* power is granted through faculties which now will probably be forwarded in certain formularies newly to be issued and communicated directly to the Ordinaries; *implicit* power belongs to those who partake of the faculties by virtue of their office, *e. g.,* Vicars General. Implicit concession is furthermore granted by the *" caput liceat "* of the Council of Trent,[8] which empowers Ordinaries to dispense in all cases of irregularity and suspension which arise from a secret crime, with the exception of voluntary homicide and such crimes as have been brought before the episcopal court by citation.

The class of cases mentioned in the second part of our canon may also be said to afford an *ordinary reason* for which those inferior to the Pope can dispense from the common law.

Three conditions must concur to make a dispensation valid[9] and licit: recourse to the Holy See must be dif-

8 Sess. 24, c. 6 de ref.

9 The canon simply says " ne-

queunt," which might be restricted to licitness; yet because dispensa-

ficult, there must be danger of grave damage, and the case must be subject to dispensation. The concurrence of these conditions may especially be verified in matrimonial cases, but also in irregularities arising from a hidden defect or crime. By *recourse to the Holy See* is here understood ordinary recourse, *i. e.*, by mail, not by telegraph, which is an extraordinary means of communication. A *grave danger* is present when escape is almost, not entirely, impossible, and hence it is not necessary that it be a *casus fortuitus,* or unforeseen incident.[10] How grave the danger must be, cannot be determined by a general rule; but scandal·or injury of reputation would suffice to constitute a serious danger. Finally, the case must be one from which the *Holy See* is wont *to dispense,* for nothing is included in the general concession which the superior is not likely to grant.[11] Hence, whatever is rare, extraordinary, unusual, or difficult to obtain from the Holy See, does not come within the sphere of episcopal power, for instance, irregularities *in defectu corporis enormi*. This is the viewpoint which the Ordinaries — and religious superiors also, for the canon does not add " *loci* " or " *locorum* "— must take in relation to the common law as contained in the Code.

The next canon deals with the power of Ordinaries regarding *diocesan laws* and laws *of provincial councils.*

CAN. 82

Episcopi aliique locorum Ordinarii dispensare valent

tions must be strictly interpreted, and because " negatio plus tollit quam affirmatio ponit," we believe that the interpretation given above is correct.

10 Barbosa, *Tractatus Varii*, p. 278, p. 108.

11 Regula juris in 6°; Reiffen-

stuel, *Comment in Reg. Iuris;* Putzer, *l. c.,* p. 36 f., enumerates still other cases, but with the exception of *dubium juris or facti* (cfr. can. 15) these cannot now be admitted, because the Code is silent about them.

in legibus dioecesanis, et in legibus Concilii provincialis ac plenarii ad normam can. 291, § 2, non vero in legibus quas speciatim tulerit Romanus Pontifex pro illo peculiari territorio, nisi ad normam can. 81.

Bishops and other diocesan Ordinaries can dispense from diocesan laws and from the laws of provincial and plenary councils, according to the rule contained in canon 291, § 2, but not from laws specially given by the Roman Pontiff for that territory, except in conformity with canon 81.

There is a gradation in this canon as to the power of dispensing. Bishops can dispense from their own (diocesan) laws with or without reason, for of their own laws they are the lawgivers in the proper sense. The second class of laws referred to comprises those of provincial or plenary councils whose decrees are supposed, according to canon 291, to be recognized by the Holy See. From these the *Ordinarii locorum* cannot licitly dispense except in particular cases and for just reasons. Now a particular case is one which occurs less frequently, and, generally speaking, touches single persons or parishes. For to dispense a whole diocese or province, if it should happen at stated or frequent intervals, would be a general not a particular dispensation. Thus to dispense the whole clergy would also be a general dispensation. Finally, the canon adds that the Ordinaries cannot dispense from particular laws given by the Holy See for that particular territory; for instance, from the law governing the nomination of candidates for vacant sees in the United States (S. C. Cons., July 25, 1916), or, perhaps, from the law regarding holy-days. The clause, however, permits dispensation in accordance with canon 81.

Descending in the scale of the hierarchy the Code says:

CAN. 83

Parochi nec a lege generali nec a lege peculiari dispensare valent, nisi haec potestas expresse eisdem concessa sit.

Parish priests can dispense neither from a general nor from a particular law, unless they have expressly received that power.

This text states an obvious truth, and at the same time deals a blow to a certain tendency which permitted *parochi ex consuetudine* to dispense in several cases.[12] For the law requires an explicit communication of that power. If parish priests need a dispensation from a general law, as embodied in our Code, the faculty must come from the Pope, either directly or indirectly through the Ordinary; if a particular law is to be dispensed from, a distinction must be made. If the law in question has been enacted by a plenary council, the habitual faculty of dispensing therefrom must be obtained from the Pope, either immediately or mediately, as in the case of the general law. For single cases, we believe, the bishops can without special faculties communicate the power of dispensing to their parish priests, for they have received this power by law (can. 291), and not from man. To dispense from merely diocesan laws depends exclusively on the bishop, who may therefore grant that faculty, either habitually or *ad certum numerum casuum,* to parish

12 Cfr. Putzer, *l. c.,* p. 36, as to dispensations from fast and ab-stinence; servile work prohibited; see can. 1245.

priests. However, it must be done expressly, either orally or in writing, and must not be presumed, for a presumption is no express concession.

After having determined the persons who may exercise the power of dispensation, the Code emphatically reinforces the Tridentine decree concerning the causes of dispensation:

CAN. 84

§ 1. A lege ecclesiastica ne dispensetur sine iusta et rationabili causa, habita ratione gravitatis legis a qua dispensatur; alias dispensatio ab inferiore data illicita et invalida est.

§ 2. Dispensatio in dubio de sufficientia causae licite petitur et potest licite et valide concedi.

§ 1. No dispensation from an ecclesiastical law is to be granted without a just and reasonable cause, and due regard must always be had to the importance of the law from which the dispensation is given; otherwise the dispensation given by an inferior is illicit and invalid.

§ 2. When there is doubt as to the sufficiency of the cause, a dispensation may be lawfully asked for, and licitly and validly granted.

The *cause* may be the motive or impelling reason, the former being the *raison d'être* of the dispensation, the latter only an aid, or, as the Scholastics express it: the motive cause is "*ad esse simpliciter*," the impelling cause, "*ad facilius esse*." Here the *causa* must be understood as the *motive* cause.[18]

---

18 If one reason is sufficient, two reasons perhaps convince: "rationes duae vincunt unam." Barbosa, *Tractatus Varii*, Axioma 197, *l. c.*, p. 130.

Concerning the *time* when the *causa* must be verified, we refer to Can. 41 *de rescriptis:* If no executor is appointed, the cause must exist at the time of granting the dispensation; if an executor handles the dispensation, the cause must be verified at the moment of his signature.

As to the *nature* of the cause, the Code says that it must be *just and reasonable.* Justice refers to law, which admits certain causes and rejects others. Thus a list of canonical causes is set up, *e. g.,* for matrimonial dispensations. The cause must be reasonable because, as law pertains to reason, so also must a dispensation partake of reason. The judgment as to the latter quality lies with the grantor.

Furthermore there must be a *proportion* between the seriousness or importance of the law and the dispensation, which is a *vulnus legis.* Hence for relaxing a serious law a serious and solid reason must be advanced; a graver cause is required to dispense from a major impediment than from a minor.[14]

Besides, it is but just that the persons should be considered for whom a dispensation is issued, because influential persons are more important for the public welfare than ordinary mortals.[15]

Lastly, the *circumstances* must be considered, not only of persons, but also of consequences which might probably follow, *e. g.,* scandal, damage, injury, etc. If the reason alleged is not just and reasonable, the dispensation granted by an inferior is illicit and invalid. Notice that the canon does not say, as the Tridentine Decree did (Sess. 25, c. 18) that it is subreptitious; hence there can be no longer any doubt as to the view taken by the Church. Therefore, if, after the application of a dis-

14 Cfr. can. 1042 f.   15 Cfr. Putzer, *l. c.,* p. 76 f.

pensation, the alleged cause is found to be without foundation, the dispensation is null and void (with the exception
of can. 1054).

§ 2 mitigates the apparent harshness of § 1, inasmuch
as it declares that, if the sufficiency of the reason alleged
is doubtful, the dispensation holds.

The next canon treats of the *interpretation* of dispensations.

CAN. 85

**Strictae subest interpretationi non solum dispensatio
ad normam can. 50, sed ipsamet facultas dispensandi
ad certum casum concessa.**

Dispensations must be strictly interpreted, according to canon 50; also the faculty of dispensing granted for a certain case is subject to
strict interpretation.

In order not to repeat what has been said before, we
only remind the reader of the rule that dispensations
must never be extended to cases and persons not comprised in the faculties, as will be further explained in
matrimonial cases. But other dispensations, too, *e. g.*
from vows, must be strictly interpreted; thus the power
of dispensing from vows does not include that of dispensing from oaths. Besides, the *clausulae* and the
stylus Curiae must be closely observed.[16] Canon 85
further mentions dispensations granted *ad certum casum*.
Here, *a fortiori*, extension of restriction is inadmis-
sible, because no argument from *dispositio similis* can
be drawn, *e. g.*, if one receives the faculty to dispense
a certain person, this cannot be applied to another, although he or she be similarly situated.

16 Cf. Putzer, *l. c.*, p. 12 f., p. 165 f.

The term "*facultas*" must be strictly interpreted in a determined case, for the general supposition is that there are personal qualities, as well as a mandate implied, which are subject to strict interpretation. The last canon treats of the *cessation* of dispensations.

Can. 86

Dispensatio quae tractum habet successivum, cessat iisdem modis quibus privilegium, nec non certa ac totali cessatione causae motivae.

A dispensation which permits of successive application ceases the same way as privileges, and with the certain and complete cessation of the motive cause.

What has been said concerning the manner in which privileges cease, must be applied here also, because habitual faculties are numbered among the *privileges beyond the law* (can. 66, § 1), and hence cease by renunciation, repeal, or the death of the grantor, if there is a clause that says so, otherwise not. To ask whether a dispensation can be lost by contrary usage and prescription seems, at first sight at least, silly. Yet a dispensation which permits of successive application (*tractum successivum*), *e. g.*, eating flesh-meat, saying a "black Mass," etc., is not exhausted by one act and may therefore be forfeited, if contrary usage and an imperative act of the superior combine. Since the Code says that such dispensations lose their force in the same way as privileges, we must apply that disposition of the law also to the case in hand.

Finally, the Code provides that if the motive cause ceases entirely and for certain, the dispensation also ceases. The two conditions ("entirely and for certain ") must be taken conjointly. For instance, if one has received a dispensation from the vow of chastity *ad usum matrimonii* on account of temptations, he may continue the use of marriage even after the cessation of these temptations, because there is no certainty. But if one has obtained a dispensation from reciting the Breviary on account of weak eyes, he cannot continue the use of the dispensation after his eyesight has been completely restored. Taking into consideration can. 85, regarding a faculty given for a determined case, the dispensation last mentioned must be held to be exhausted after application, and is therefore *negotium finitum*. For it is generally supposed that in such a case the faculty was given in *forma mandati*, which expires after application and admits of no extension or *epikia*.

www.ingramcontent.com/pod-product-compliance
Lightning Source LLC
LaVergne TN
LVHW050151060326
832904LV00003B/117